The Ubiquitous Shrimp

The Ubiquitous Shrimp

Judith Choate

PHOTOGRAPHY BY BILL MILNE

LITTLE, BROWN AND COMPANY

BOSTON NEW YORK TORONTO LONDON

First Edition

ISBN 0-316-13928-9

Library of Congress Cataloging-in-Publication Data
Choate, Judith.
    The ubiquitous shrimp / Judith Choate.—1st ed.
        p.   cm.
    Includes index.
    ISBN 0-316-13928-9
    1. Cookery (Shrimp) 2. Cookery. International.   I. Title.
TX754.S58C48 1993
641.6'95—dc20   93-4525

A KENAN BOOK

THE UBIQUITOUS SHRIMP
was prepared and produced by
Kenan Books, Inc.
15 West 26th Street
New York, NY 10010

Editor: Dana Rosen
Art Director: Jeff Batzli
Designer: Susan Livingston
Photography Director: Christopher Bain
All photographs ©Bill Milne 1993
Food Stylist: A.J. Battifarano
Prop Stylist: Lynn McMahill

10 9 8 7 6 5 4 3 2 1

Printed in Hong Kong and bound in China
by Leefung-Asco Printers Ltd.

DEDICATION

For Aris Mixon—

Just 'cause he loves shrimp

INTRODUCTION

8

Buying Shrimp
9

Preparing Shrimp
10

**Basic Cooking
Instructions**
12

CHAPTER I

Hors d'Oeuvres
and Appetizers

14

CHAPTER II

Hot and Cold
Soups

48

CHAPTER III

Sensational
Salads

6 2

CHAPTER IV

Main
Courses

8 4

CHAPTER V

Spices and
Sauce Mixes

1 1 8

INDEX

126

Introduction

Whether it is a huge bowl of chilled shrimp served with a fabulous spicy sauce; a cool, thinning summer salad; or an elegant main course featuring giant, pale pink prawns, the shrimp is America's favorite seafood. Eaten alone or as a tasty bonus in almost any recipe, shrimp will turn the most mundane meal into a special feast.

Shrimp is most often used as a generic term for prawns, langoustines, crawfish, and small lobsters as well as the ten-legged crustacean that is the true shrimp. Ranging in size from microscopic to the giant shrimp found in the Mexican Gulf and along the coast of the Pacific Northwest, there are, in fact, hundreds of species located throughout the world. They are found in salty or fresh water, warm or icy water, and in the muddy bottoms of the shallows or floating in the deep. Whatever its home waters may be, this flavorful crustacean, although somewhat high in cholesterol, is a superb low-fat, low-calorie source of protein, vitamins, and minerals.

Shrimp did not become available to the home cook until well into the twentieth century; because it is an exceptionally perishable foodstuff, it could not be brought to the table quickly enough until the advent of refrigerated fishing trawlers in the late 1920s. There were, of course, coastal areas where local fishermen could swiftly bring their harvest to the cook. Charleston, South Carolina, has long been famous for its early morning shrimp criers announcing their briny catch, and the New Orleans Shrimp Boil is deeply embedded in American culinary lore.

Throughout the world are coastal or island shrimp dishes, found in such diverse cuisines as those of China, Japan, Africa, and Scandinavia. The recent wide availability of shrimp has expanded the variety of recipes that include this mellow seafood.

The Ubiquitous Shrimp brings together all of these recipes, from the simplest to the most exotic, from feasts to snacks. Easy to cook, versatile, adaptable to any cuisine, and delicious to eat, the ubiquitous shrimp should indeed be on every table.

BUYING SHRIMP

Fresh raw shrimp should be quite firm and free of any strong odor, with the shell somewhat crisp yet flexible. They are most frequently sold with the head and thorax removed; you are, therefore, actually buying shrimp tails. However, the liver, commonly called the tomalley, is located in the head and is, in some cuisines, a very desirable addition to a shrimp meal.

Although shrimp are available year-round, they are usually most expensive from January until the beginning of May. Frozen raw shrimp are available in the freezer section of most supermarkets, but if you can find them, fresh shrimp are more flavorful and crisp to the bite. However, since for most cooks frozen shrimp are the only ones available, use them just as you would the fresh shrimp called for in these recipes.

Raw shrimp are sized according to the number required to make a pound. The general categories are: giant, approximately ten per pound; jumbo, approximately fifteen per pound; large, approximately twenty per pound; medium, approximately thirty per pound; and small, approximately forty per pound. Prawns are often sold as large shrimp, although scientifically they should not be so categorized. However, the name "prawn" has also come to mean the largest commercially available shrimp. All of this can be rather confusing to the home cook, so whether called shrimp or prawns, these large, succulent creatures can be used interchangeably in any recipe.

The size of the shrimp will not necessarily determine its taste. However, the color frequently will. The pink color we associate with shrimp is caused by its iodine content. Therefore, the deeper the color, the stronger the iodine taste will be, with the deep brownish-pink shrimp usually having the strongest iodine flavor. The two most commonly available shrimp are either pale pink or creamy white. There are, however, also many exotically striped and spotted varieties that can occasionally be found in the marketplace.

It is most economical to purchase raw shrimp in the shell. Shelling and cooking will, of course, cause a significant weight loss, so you will need to allow more weight per portion than you would normally allow when buying fish fillets or meat. For instance, if using jumbo shrimp for a main course, you will want about six to eight, or approximately one-half pound, per person.

Fresh raw shrimp should be prepared on the day of purchase. If the shrimp won't be prepared for several hours, rinse them under cold running water and pat dry. Wrap in a cool, damp paper towel; place in a plastic bag, plastic film, or a nonabsorbent container (such as glass); and seal tightly. Refrigerate until ready to use. Do not use fresh shrimp that is more than two days old. If you cannot use freshly purchased shrimp, remove the heads, rinse well, and pat dry. Then wrap tightly and seal in a nonabsorbent container and freeze for up to three months.

PREPARING SHRIMP

Shrimp can be cooked before or after shelling. If using shrimp in the shell, they should simply be rinsed under cold running water and patted dry before cooking.

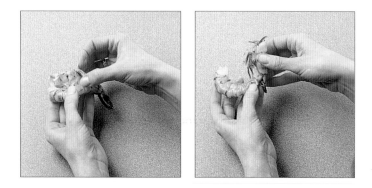

To shell shrimp, either before or after cooking, first pull off the legs. Then strip off the shell by peeling it back from the leg area. The tail can be removed or left on depending on the recipe requirements.

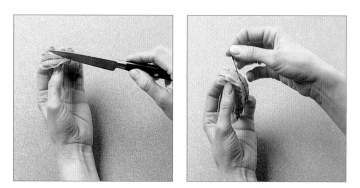

To devein or not is an age-old shrimp cook's question. It is truly a matter of aesthetics rather than necessity. The black vein running down the back of the shrimp is, in fact, its digestive tract and can be quite gritty. I prefer to remove the vein with a small paring knife and then rinse the shrimp under cold running water. (You may also purchase an inexpensive shrimp-deveining gadget, which is available at most kitchen supply stores.) Always pat the shrimp dry before using.

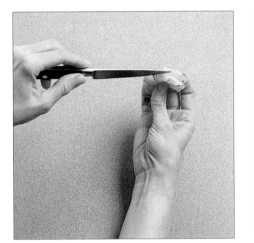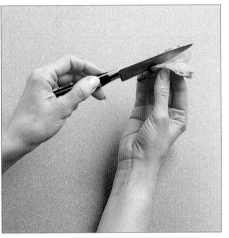

To butterfly shrimp, shell and devein it, leaving the tail on. Using a sharp knife, make a shallow cut down the center of the underside but not through the shrimp. Lay the shrimp open, deveined side up, and make shallow cuts diagonally out from the center on both sides.

If using a recipe that requires a court bouillon or a fish stock, use the shrimp shells for additional flavor in the stock.

To rid shrimp of a strong iodine flavor, soak the unshelled shrimp in a solution of 2 tablespoons baking soda dissolved in 1 quart cold water for 10 minutes. Drain and rinse thoroughly under cold running water before proceeding with preparation.

BASIC COOKING INSTRUCTIONS

Shrimp is truly one of the most versatile seafoods. It is prepared using almost every cooking method and in almost every cuisine, as well as being eaten raw in Japan. However, there are some simple basic methods that make shrimp especially easy to prepare for a quick meal.

SIMPLE BOILED SHRIMP

This method is best used for shrimp that will be further enhanced with a sauce. For every pound of shrimp, bring 4 cups cold water to a boil. Add salt to taste. When the water is rapidly boiling, add the shrimp, either shelled or not. Allow to simmer for about 3 minutes or until they are firm, opaque, and curled. Drain and rinse under cold running water. Shell, if necessary. Pat dry.

SHRIMP BOILED IN COURT BOUILLON

Combine 2 quarts water; 1½ cups white wine; 1 lemon, quartered; 2 stalks celery, washed, trimmed, and chopped; 1 small onion, peeled and studded with 6 whole cloves; 6 sprigs parsley; 1 teaspoon white peppercorns; 1 bay leaf; pinch each of fennel and anise seeds; salt to taste. Bring to a boil. When boiling, add the shrimp and simmer for about 3 minutes or until they are firm, opaque, and curled. Serve alone or with a dipping sauce. (Do not discard the court bouillon. Use it to make a fish stock by adding some well-washed fish and/or shellfish bones, heads, and trimmings. Simmer for 1 hour. Strain and allow to cool before storing. Store, tightly covered, refrigerated for up to 1 day or frozen for up to 3 months.)

SHRIMP BOIL

There are commercially packaged shrimp (or crab) boil spices, or you can make your own (see page 124). Add to water or a combination of water and white wine and cook as directed on the container. For a traditional shrimp boil, the shrimp are cooked and served in the shell. The warm shrimp are shelled by the diner and dipped into either melted butter or a favorite dipping sauce. This informal meal is usually eaten on newspaper so that the shells can be wrapped up and easily discarded.

GRILLED SHRIMP

Use jumbo shrimp only. The shrimp should be rinsed well and patted dry, either in the shell or not, as you prefer. For every pound of shrimp, combine $\frac{1}{4}$ cup olive oil or melted butter; 1 tablespoon fresh lemon juice; 1 tablespoon minced fresh herbs (such as dill, thyme, parsley or basil); 1 tablespoon minced shallots; 1 clove garlic, peeled and minced; salt and pepper to taste. Add shrimp and toss to combine. If the shrimp are not large enough to lay on the grill without falling through, place them on skewers $\frac{1}{2}$ inch apart. Place on a hot grill or under a preheated broiler and cook for about 2 minutes per side or until they are opaque and firm to the touch. Serve hot.

DEEP-FRIED SHRIMP

Clean and shell the shrimp, leaving the tails intact. For every pound of shrimp, combine 1 cup buttermilk, $\frac{1}{2}$ teaspoon grated lemon zest, salt to taste. Add shrimp and toss to combine. Allow to soak for 10 minutes. Combine 1 cup cornmeal, $\frac{1}{2}$ cup all-purpose flour, $\frac{1}{2}$ teaspoon paprika, salt and pepper to taste. Toss the soaked shrimp in the seasoned cornmeal mixture. Let stand 15 minutes. Heat 4 cups vegetable oil to 375°F in a deep-fat fryer. When hot, coat a few shrimp and fry for about 3 minutes or until the coating is crisp and the shrimp are cooked through. Repeat coating and frying until all the shrimp are cooked. Serve hot with lemon wedges.

SAUTEED SHRIMP

Peeled and deveined shrimp can be quickly sautéed (for no more than about 4 minutes) in a small amount of hot olive oil, vegetable oil, or butter, and seasoned to taste with salt, pepper, and lemon juice, if desired.

CHAPTER 1

Hors d'Oeuvres and Appetizers

What is a more welcoming sight at a cocktail buffet than a huge iced bowl of pale pink shrimp? No other food, except perhaps an equal amount of caviar, tells your guests that they are special. There are also many hors d'oeuvre and appetizer recipes incorporating shrimp that will elicit the same response yet cost far less. A first course starring shrimp is an elegant beginning to a meal that can then feature a less costly entrée. The shrimp will be the highlight in your guests' memories and your party planning will be the model of perfection.

Do not be afraid to fill that huge iced bowl; you can never have too many shrimp. However, I suggest that you do not put all of the shrimp out at once, as you want to make sure that every guest has the opportunity to share in your bounty. For the all-time standard pre-dinner shrimp cocktail, allow five shrimp per person. For other, more intricate pre-dinner shrimp dishes, I usually allow three to four shrimp per person.

SHRIMP COCKTAIL

MAKES 1.

Chopped lettuce (optional)
**6 large or 5 jumbo shrimp, boiled, peeled,
and deveined, tails intact**
¼ cup Standard Cocktail Sauce (see page 121)
1 lemon wedge

If you have bowls made especially for shrimp cocktail, use them tightly packed with shaved ice. If not, line sherbet glasses or small bowls with chopped lettuce. Lay the shrimp in an attractive pattern on top of the lettuce. Top with cocktail sauce. Garnish with lemon wedges.

Note: Instead of topping the shrimp with the cocktail sauce, pass the cocktail sauce with horseradish, Tabasco, and fresh lemon juice on the side.

The perfect shrimp cocktail.

SHRIMP BUTTER (POTTED SHRIMP)

MAKES ABOUT 4 CUPS.

**1 pound cooked, peeled, and deveined
shrimp**
2 cups clarified butter (see Note on page 35)
2 tablespoons minced fresh parsley
1 tablespoon minced fresh ginger
1 teaspoon grated lemon zest

Place all ingredients in a food processor fitted with the metal blade. Process until smooth. Scrape into a 1-quart terrine or other glass container. Cover and refrigerate until ready to use.

Note: This is a wonderful spread for freshly toasted homemade white or rye bread.

SHRIMP WITH SNOW PEAS AND PROSCIUTTO

SERVES 6 TO 8.

1½ pounds large cooked, peeled, and deveined shrimp, tails intact

¾ cup extra-virgin olive oil

¼ cup champagne vinegar or other fine white-wine vinegar

1 tablespoon Dijon-style mustard

1 tablespoon minced shallots

1 tablespoon minced fresh ginger

1 tablespoon minced fresh cilantro

1 teaspoon fresh lime juice

½ teaspoon minced fresh green chili pepper (or to taste)

Pinch of sugar

Salt to taste

15 to 20 snow peas

¼ pound thinly sliced prosciutto

Combine shrimp with oil, vinegar, mustard, shallots, ginger, cilantro, lime juice, chilies, sugar, and salt. Pour shrimp mixture into a nonreactive container. Cover and refrigerate for 12 hours, turning it occasionally.

Immerse peas in boiling water for about 20 seconds or until just pliable but still bright green. Drain immediately and refresh in iced water. Drain and pat dry. String peas and pull apart lengthwise into halves.

Remove shrimp from marinade and lay on paper towels to drain slightly. Wrap a small piece of prosciutto around each shrimp. Wrap half a pea pod around each shrimp. Fasten pea pod to shrimp by sticking a wooden toothpick through the overlap. Cover and refrigerate until ready to serve.

POACHED SHRIMP WITH POBLANO PESTO

SERVES 6 TO 8.

2 pounds large shrimp
2 cups water
2 cups dry white wine
2 carrots, peeled and chopped
1 onion, peeled and chopped
1 fennel bulb, washed and chopped
1 jalapeño chili pepper (or to taste), washed and halved
3 cloves garlic, peeled
1 large piece orange rind
1 teaspoon black peppercorns
Poblano Pesto

Peel shrimp, leaving tails on and reserving the shells. Place shells and remaining ingredients, except pesto, in a stock pot over high heat. Bring to a boil; boil for 20 minutes. Remove from heat and strain, reserving the liquid.

Return the liquid to the pot over high heat. Bring to a boil. When boiling, add the shrimp. Lower heat and simmer for about 2 minutes or until shrimp are just opaque. Drain well. Pat the shrimp dry.

Arrange shrimp on a serving platter, tails out. Place Poblano Pesto in a bowl in the center of the platter. Serve cold.

Note: For parties you may want to garnish the platter with greens or herb sprigs.

POBLANO PESTO

MAKES ABOUT 2 CUPS.

6 poblano chili peppers, roasted and seeded
½ cup toasted, unsalted macadamia nuts, pine nuts, or walnuts
1 cup tightly packed cilantro leaves
1 teaspoon minced fresh mint
2 cloves garlic, peeled
⅓ cup extra-virgin olive oil
¼ cup fresh lime juice
1 tablespoon fresh orange juice
Salt to taste

Place the poblanos, nuts, cilantro, mint, garlic, and oil in a food processor fitted with the metal blade. Puree, using quick on-and-off turns, until the mixture is smooth. Add citrus juices and salt; pulse to combine. Taste and adjust seasoning, if necessary. Pour into a nonreactive bowl. Cover and refrigerate until ready to use.

SHRIMP PÂTÉ WITH AVOCADO-DILL SAUCE

MAKES 1 LOAF.

12 to 16 large spinach leaves
2 pounds large peeled shrimp
1½ cups heavy cream
1 large egg white
Cayenne pepper to taste
Salt to taste
Pinch ground nutmeg
Avocado-Dill Sauce
Rye toast triangles or rye crackers

Preheat oven to 350°F.

Butter a 1-quart terrine or loaf pan. Carefully devein spinach leaves. Quickly dip into boiling water to just wilt. Pat dry. Line buttered terrine with spinach leaves, leaving enough overhang around the edges to pull up and fold over the top.

Place shrimp, cream, egg white, cayenne, salt, and nutmeg in a food processor fitted with the metal blade. Puree, using quick on-and-off turns.

Bring a small amount of water to boil. Place a spoonful of the shrimp mixture in the boiling water. Poach for a minute or two, until just cooked. Taste and adjust seasoning, if necessary.

Scrape the shrimp mixture into the spinach-lined terrine. Tamp down and smooth the top. Bring the spinach leaves over the top to cover the pâté. Place a piece of buttered parchment paper over the top. Tightly seal the entire terrine with heavy-duty aluminum foil. Place the terrine in a larger pan with enough water to come up about 1½ inches. Bake for 15 minutes or until the internal temperature reaches 120°F on a food thermometer.

Remove from oven and cool on a wire rack. When cool, refrigerate for at least 1 hour, or overnight. Unmold and cut into thin slices. Serve with Avocado-Dill Sauce and rye toast or crackers.

Note: Serve as an appetizer with 2 to 3 slices per person, napping the slices with Avocado-Dill Sauce and sprinkling the top with salmon caviar and chopped chives.

Shrimp Pâté with Avocado-Dill Sauce
garnished with whole shrimp, radicchio, and mâche.

SHRIMP NACHOS

SERVES 6 TO 8.

12 shrimp, cooked, peeled, deveined, and
   chopped
½ cup finely diced mango
¼ cup finely diced avocado
¼ cup finely diced yellow bell peppers
2 tablespoons grated sweet onions
1 clove garlic, peeled and minced
1 tablespoon minced fresh cilantro
1 tablespoon minced fresh mint
1 serrano chili pepper, roasted, peeled, and
   seeded
2 tablespoons fresh lime juice
2 tablespoons canola oil
   Salt to taste
   Pepper to taste
48 blue corn chips
¼ cup grated Monterey Jack cheese

Combine shrimp with mango, avocado, peppers, onions, garlic, cilantro, and mint. Mash the chili and combine with lime juice and oil. When well blended, stir into shrimp mixture. Add salt and pepper and toss to combine.

Preheat broiler.

Place about 1 tablespoon of the shrimp mixture in the center of each corn chip. Sprinkle with cheese. Lay chips on broiler tray and broil for about 30 seconds or until cheese is just melted. Serve immediately.

AVOCADO-DILL SAUCE

MAKES ABOUT 1½ CUPS.

1 ripe avocado, peeled and seeded
   (see Note)
¼ cup nonfat unflavored yogurt
¼ cup sour cream
   Juice of 1 lemon
¼ cup minced fresh dill
   Tabasco sauce to taste
   Salt to taste

Puree the avocado with the yogurt and sour cream in a food processor fitted with the metal blade. Scrape into a nonreactive bowl and stir in remaining ingredients. Taste and adjust seasoning, if necessary. Cover and refrigerate until ready to serve.

Note: If preparing the sauce ahead of time, save the avocado pit and place it in the center of the sauce in order to help prevent discoloration.

COCONUT SHRIMP WITH GINGER DIPPING SAUCE

SERVES 6 TO 8.

- 1½ **pounds large shrimp, peeled and deveined, tails intact**
- 3 **large eggs**
- 2 **tablespoons water**
- 1 **tablespoon fresh lime juice**
- 1 **tablespoon Tabasco sauce or other hot-pepper sauce**
-   **Salt to taste**
- 3 **cups unflavored bread crumbs**
- 1 **cup all-purpose flour**
- 2 **cups shredded sweetened coconut**
- 1 **teaspoon cayenne pepper**
-   **About 6 cups vegetable oil**
-   **Ginger Dipping Sauce**

Wash shrimp and pat dry.

Whisk together eggs, water, lime juice, hot-pepper sauce, and salt. Line a baking sheet with waxed paper. Combine bread crumbs, flour, coconut, and cayenne. Holding shrimp by the tail, dip into the egg mixture. Then roll in coconut mixture to coat well. Place the coated shrimp on the lined baking sheet. When all the shrimp are coated, cover lightly and refrigerate for 1 hour.

Heat oil in a deep-sided pan or deep-fryer until it reaches 375°F on a food thermometer. When hot, add shrimp in small batches. Fry for about 3 minutes or until golden. Drain on paper towels. Serve hot with Ginger Dipping Sauce.

GINGER DIPPING SAUCE

MAKES 2 CUPS.

- 1 **cup light soy sauce**
- ½ **cup orange marmalade**
- ¼ **cup minced fresh ginger**
- ¼ **cup rice-wine vinegar***
-   ***Available in Asian or gourmet markets.***

Combine all ingredients in a small saucepan over medium heat. Bring to a boil. When boiling, immediately remove from heat and allow to rest for 30 minutes. Strain into a serving bowl and serve at room temperature.

SHRIMP CUERNAVACA

SERVES 6 TO 8.

½ pound shrimp, peeled and deveined

1 teaspoon canola oil

2 teaspoons minced fresh dill

1 teaspoon minced fresh cilantro

1 tablespoon fresh lemon juice

1 tablespoon fresh lime juice

¾ cup diced avocado

2 tablespoons minced red bell peppers

1 tablespoon Dijon-style mustard

Tabasco sauce to taste

Salt to taste

White pepper to taste

24 large fresh mushroom caps

1 cup grated Monterey Jack cheese or queso blanco*

Available in Latin American or gourmet markets.

Rinse shrimp and pat dry.

Heat oil in medium sauté pan over medium heat. When hot, add shrimp, dill, and cilantro. Stir to coat. Then add citrus juices. Sauté, stirring constantly, for about 3 minutes or until shrimp are opaque. Remove from pan and allow to cool.

Preheat oven to 450°F.

Chop shrimp and place in a small bowl. Add avocado, red peppers, mustard, Tabasco, salt, and pepper. Stir to combine. When well combined, spoon mixture into mushroom caps, mounding slightly. Sprinkle with cheese. Place on a baking sheet and bake for about 4 minutes or until the mushrooms are slightly softened and the cheese has melted. Serve warm.

Shrimp Cuernavaca.

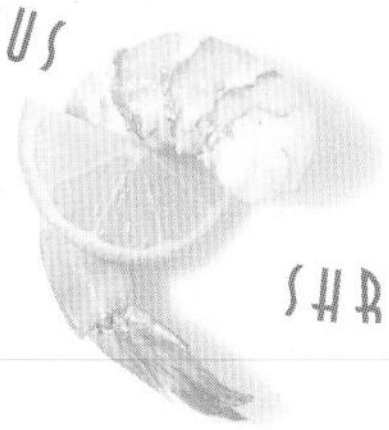

SHRIMP PAN ROAST

SERVES 6.

1½ pounds medium shrimp, peeled and deveined

⅓ cup extra-virgin olive oil

¼ cup fish stock (see page 12)

2 tablespoons Pernod

2 tablespoons white-wine vinegar

1 tablespoon fresh lime juice

3 shallots, peeled and minced

¼ cup minced fresh chives

2 tablespoons minced fresh parsley

1 tablespoon minced fresh marjoram or 1 teaspoon dried

Salt to taste

Pepper to taste

12 diagonal slices baguette, toasted

¼ cup finely diced red bell peppers

Place shrimp in an ovenproof glass baking dish. Add oil, fish stock, Pernod, vinegar, lime juice, shallots, herbs, salt, and pepper. Cover and refrigerate for at least 4 hours to marinate. When marinated, return to room temperature.

Preheat broiler.

Place shrimp under preheated broiler and cook for 3 minutes or until opaque and curled.

Place 2 pieces of toast on each of 6 small serving plates. Spoon equal portions of shrimp on each plate. Sprinkle with peppers and serve immediately.

SHRIMP FRITTERS WITH GARLIC SAUCE

SERVES 6 TO 8.

2 pounds large shrimp, cooked, peeled, and deveined
1 cup cooked mashed potatoes
2 large eggs, lightly beaten
2 tablespoons all-purpose flour
½ teaspoon baking powder
1 tablespoon minced fresh dill
1 tablespoon minced fresh parsley
1 tablespoon minced shallots
1 teaspoon fresh lemon juice
Tabasco sauce to taste
Salt to taste
About 6 cups vegetable oil
Garlic Sauce

Finely chop shrimp. Combine with potatoes, eggs, flour, baking powder, dill, parsley, shallots, lemon juice, Tabasco, and salt.

Heat oil in deep-fat fryer until it reaches 375°F on a food thermometer. When hot, drop shrimp batter by the tablespoon into the oil. Fry for about 3 minutes or until cooked through and golden. Remove from oil and drain on paper towels. Serve hot with Garlic Sauce.

GARLIC SAUCE

MAKES ABOUT 1½ CUPS.

⅔ cup mayonnaise
⅓ cup sour cream
6 scallions, white parts only, chopped
6 cloves garlic, peeled
3 tablespoons chopped fresh dill
2 tablespoons chopped fresh parsley
2 tablespoons fresh orange juice
1 teaspoon grated orange zest
Salt to taste
Pepper to taste

Place all ingredients in a food processor fitted with the metal blade. Process, using quick on-and-off turns, until blended. Taste and adjust seasoning with salt and pepper, if necessary. Cover and refrigerate for at least 1 hour before using.

SHRIMP DUMPLINGS WITH DIPPING SAUCE

SERVES 6.

½ **pound shrimp, peeled, deveined, and finely minced**
½ **cup minced water chestnuts**
1 **tablespoon black sesame seeds***
1 **tablespoon minced fresh cilantro**
2 **teaspoons minced shallots**
1 **teaspoon minced fresh parsley**
½ **teaspoon minced fresh ginger**
1 **egg white, lightly beaten**
1 **teaspoon sherry**
1 **teaspoon sesame oil***
1 **teaspoon light soy sauce (or to taste)**
30 **wonton wrappers***
8 **large lettuce leaves**
  Dipping Sauce
  Available in Asian or gourmet markets.

**Shrimp Dumplings with Dipping Sauce
served in a steamer basket lined with lettuce leaves.**

Combine shrimp, water chestnuts, sesame seeds, cilantro, shallots, parsley, and ginger. Beat the egg white, sherry, sesame oil, and soy sauce. When frothy, stir into shrimp mixture.

Bring a small amount of water to a boil. Place a spoonful of the shrimp mixture in the boiling water. Poach for a minute or two, until just cooked. Taste and adjust seasoning, if necessary.

Cut wonton wrappers into 3-inch circles using a biscuit cutter or drinking glass. Cover with a damp cloth to keep them from drying out. Form the dumplings according to the directions on the following page.

Place the filled dumplings, in batches if necessary, in the top half of a bamboo steamer lined with lettuce leaves. Place the steamer over boiling water and steam for about 10 minutes or until the filling is cooked and heated through. Serve immediately with Dipping Sauce.

MAKING THE DUMPLINGS

To make the dumplings, hold a wonton wrapper in the middle of your palm and spoon about 2 teaspoons of the shrimp filling into the center. With the other hand, use your fingers to gently pleat the wonton wrapper around the filling, as shown in the center photograph. Place the dumpling on a flat, dry surface and flatten the bottom by gently tapping it down.

MY FAVORITE SCAMPI

SERVES 6.

1½ pounds shrimp, peeled and deveined, tails intact
¼ cup extra-virgin olive oil
¼ cup melted butter
¼ cup white wine
3 tablespoons minced garlic
1 tablespoon minced fresh parsley
Juice of 1 lemon
Salt to taste
Pepper to taste
Crusty Italian bread

Preheat broiler.

Combine all ingredients, except bread, in a shallow baking dish. Place under the preheated broiler and broil for about 4 minutes, stirring once or twice, or until shrimp are slightly browned.

Place 4 to 6 shrimp on each of 6 small serving plates. Divide the pan juices among the plates and serve immediately with warm bread to absorb the juices.

DIPPING SAUCE

MAKES ABOUT 1½ CUPS.

1 cup fine white vinegar
½ cup loosely packed brown sugar
¼ cup finely diced seedless cucumbers
1 serrano chili pepper (or to taste), seeded and minced
1 tablespoon minced fresh mint
1 tablespoon minced fresh cilantro
1 teaspoon grated fresh ginger
1 teaspoon fresh lime juice
Salt to taste

Combine all ingredients in a nonreactive bowl. Cover and refrigerate until ready to serve.

BLUE CHEESE SHRIMP

SERVES 6.

18 jumbo shrimp, peeled and deveined

¼ cup all-purpose flour

1 tablespoon grated orange zest

Salt to taste

Pepper to taste

1 tablespoon unsalted butter

2 tablespoons Chartreuse

1 cup heavy cream

¼ cup crème fraîche*

2 ounces Maytag Blue cheese or other fine blue cheese

1 teaspoon minced fresh thyme

18 white toast points

2 tablespoons minced fresh parsley

Available in gourmet markets.

Wash shrimp and pat dry. Combine flour, orange zest, salt, and pepper in a flat dish. Add shrimp and toss to lightly coat. Shake off any excess.

Melt butter in a large, heavy sauté pan over medium-high heat. When melted, add shrimp and sauté for about 2 minutes or until just curling and beginning to turn opaque. Add Chartreuse and cook for 1 minute. Add heavy cream, crème fraîche, blue cheese, and thyme. Cook, stirring constantly, for about 3 minutes or until the cheese is melted and the shrimp have cooked through.

Place 3 toast points on each of 6 small serving plates. Place a shrimp on top of each toast point and drizzle sauce over top. Garnish with parsley. Serve immediately.

SHRIMP CROSTINI

MAKES ABOUT 40.

1 pound shrimp, peeled and deveined
1 cup extra-virgin olive oil
3 shallots, peeled and chopped
2 tablespoons minced garlic
2 cups fresh bread crumbs
1 cup Italian parsley leaves
¼ cup freshly grated Parmesan cheese
1 tablespoon well-drained capers
1 teaspoon fresh lemon juice
  Salt to taste
  Pepper to taste
2 baguettes, sliced diagonally about
  ¼ inch thick
1 large clove garlic, peeled

Wash shrimp and pat dry.

Heat 2 tablespoons oil in a heavy sauté pan over medium-high heat. When hot, add shrimp, shallots, and minced garlic. Sauté for about 3 minutes or until shrimp has just turned pink. Scrape into a food processor fitted with the metal blade. Chop, using quick on-and-off turns. Add ⅓ cup oil, bread crumbs, parsley, cheese, capers, lemon juice, salt, and pepper and process until just combined. Do not puree.

Preheat oven to 400°F.

Using ¼ cup oil, brush each slice of bread and then rub with the garlic clove. Lay the slices on a baking sheet in a single layer. Bake for about 6 minutes or until golden. Remove from oven and spread the shrimp mixture on top of each slice. Drizzle with remaining oil and serve immediately.

SHRIMP-FILLED TOMATO CREPES WITH PEPPERED VODKA SAUCE

SERVES 6.

3 large eggs

1 serrano chili pepper, stemmed and seeded

1 cup all-purpose flour

½ teaspoon sugar

1 cup tomato juice

½ cup water

   Salt to taste

   White pepper to taste

2 tablespoons melted unsalted butter

¼ cup chilled unsalted butter

3 tablespoons peppered vodka

3 tablespoons minced shallots

¼ cup minced fresh cilantro

1 cup peeled, seeded, and diced tomatoes

¼ cup diced water chestnuts

1½ pounds cooked small shrimp, peeled and deveined, or a combination of cooked lobster and shrimp

¼ cup clarified butter (see Note)

   Peppered Vodka Sauce

6 teaspoons black caviar (optional)

To make crepe batter, process eggs and chili in a blender until chili is minced. Add flour, sugar, tomato juice, water, salt, pepper, and melted butter. Process until smooth. Pour into a medium bowl, cover, and let rest for at least 1 hour.

To make filling, melt 2 tablespoons chilled butter in a heavy sauté pan over medium-low heat. Add vodka and stir to combine. Add shallots and 1 tablespoon cilantro and cook, stirring frequently, for about 5 minutes or until shallots are very soft. Whisk in remaining chilled butter a bit at a time. When butter is incorporated, stir in tomatoes, water chestnuts, and shrimp. Remove from heat and set aside. Keep warm.

Heat a 6-inch crepe pan over medium-high heat. Brush with clarified butter. Stir crepe batter. When butter is hot, pour in about 2 tablespoons crepe batter, tilting the pan as you pour, to cover the bottom. The crepe should set almost immediately, and the bottom should be brown in about 1 minute. Check by lifting an edge. Flip the crepe over and brown the other side. Stack

cooked crepes and keep them warm as you cook remaining batter. This recipe allows enough batter for breakage. You will need 12 crepes, allowing 2 per person.

When crepes are ready, fill each one with an equal portion of shrimp filling. Fold sides in to enclose filling.

Preheat oven to 350°F.

Use clarified butter to generously grease a baking dish large enough to hold the crepes. Lay crepes in the prepared pan, seam side down. Cover with aluminum foil and bake for 10 minutes. Remove from oven and place 2 crepes on each of 6 warm plates. Spoon Peppered Vodka Sauce over the crepes and sprinkle with the remaining minced cilantro and a spoonful of caviar, if desired. Serve immediately.

Note: To clarify butter, melt cold butter over low heat. When melted, allow to sit about 5 minutes and then pour clear yellow liquid off and discard the solids. Use the clarified butter immediately or cover tightly and store refrigerated for 1 week or frozen for 6 months.

PEPPERED VODKA SAUCE

MAKES ABOUT 1 CUP.

- ½ **cup peppered vodka**
- ½ **teaspoon fresh lemon juice**
- 3 **tablespoons minced shallots**
- 2 **tablespoons minced fresh cilantro**
- ½ **teaspoon salt (or to taste)**
- ½ **teaspoon white pepper**
- 3 **large egg yolks**
- 1 **cup melted unsalted butter**

Place vodka, lemon juice, shallots, cilantro, salt, and pepper in a small, heavy saucepan over medium-high heat. Cook for about 5 minutes or until reduced to 2 tablespoons. Place in a blender or food processor, add the egg yolks, and use quick on-and-off turns to just combine. With the motor running, add butter in a steady stream. When well combined, remove from blender; do not overmix. Pour into a microwave-safe container and microwave on medium for 1 minute. Whisk well. (Sauce will appear curdled, but whisking will smooth it.)

SHRIMP SPRING ROLLS WITH SPICY DIPPING SAUCE

MAKES ABOUT 30 ROLLS.

1 package (about 1.7 ounces) cellophane noodles (also called bean thread noodles)*

5 dried Chinese mushrooms*

¼ cup dried tree ears (also called cloud ears or tree fungus)*

¾ pound shrimp, peeled, deveined, and coarsely chopped

¼ pound boneless, skinless chicken breast, coarsely chopped

¾ cup bean sprouts, coarsely chopped

¾ cup shredded carrots

4 scallions, chopped

2 cloves garlic, peeled and minced

1 tablespoon minced cilantro stems

1 large egg

2 tablespoons fish sauce (such as nuoc nam or nam pla)*

White pepper to taste

1 cup sugar

1 package rice paper sheets or wonton wrappers*

About 6 cups vegetable oil

2 heads Boston or Bibb lettuce, washed, dried, and pulled apart

1 cucumber, peeled, seeded, and julienned

1 cup cilantro leaves

1 cup mint leaves

Spicy Dipping Sauce

Available in Asian or gourmet markets.

Place cellophane noodles, mushrooms, and tree ears in separate bowls large enough to hold enough hot water to allow them to expand without crowding. Cover each with hot water and allow to soften. When soft, drain each thoroughly, squeezing out excess water, then coarsely chop and place in a large mixing bowl. Add the shrimp, chicken, and bean sprouts to the noodle mixture. Stir in carrots, scallions, garlic, and cilantro. Add the egg, fish sauce, and pepper. Mix until well combined.

Shrimp Spring Rolls with Spicy Dipping Sauce.

If using rice paper sheets, combine sugar with about 6 cups hot water in a large, shallow pan wide enough to allow 1 sheet of rice paper to be completely submerged. Stir to dissolve sugar. Place a clean, damp kitchen towel next to the pan. Submerge 1 sheet of rice paper at a time and allow it to soak for about 30 seconds or until soft and pliable. Remove from water and allow excess water to drip off. Lay on damp kitchen towel. Make spring rolls as directed at right.

MAKING A SPRING ROLL

Fold up the bottom third of a soft rice paper sheet or wonton wrapper. Place 3 tablespoons of the filling on the folded-over portion a bit up from the bottom. Fold the bottom over the filling and fold the sides of the rice sheet over the top to enclose the filling. Gently roll the filled rice sheet or wonton wrapper into a tight cylinder.

Line a baking sheet with paper towels. Place the finished spring rolls, seamside down, on the paper towels. Continue until all the filling and rice sheets are used.

Heat about 3 inches of oil in a deep-fat fryer or wok to about 350°F on a food thermometer. When oil is hot, fry spring rolls, a few at a time, for about 8 to 10 minutes or until golden and the filling is cooked through. Drain on paper towels and keep warm until ready to serve.

To serve, cut each roll in half on the diagonal. Place on a serving platter or on individual plates with lettuce, cucumber, cilantro, and mint. Pass Spicy Dipping Sauce separately.

Note: To eat the spring rolls, place a half in a lettuce leaf, add a few cilantro leaves, a few mint leaves, and a few pieces of cucumber. Roll the lettuce leaf around the spring roll and dip into the sauce as you eat.

SPICY DIPPING SAUCE

MAKES ABOUT 1½ CUPS.

½ cup water
½ cup rice-wine vinegar*
⅓ cup fish sauce (such as nuoc nam or nam pla)*
¼ cup fresh lime juice
3 tablespoons sugar
2 tablespoons minced garlic
1 small serrano chili pepper, seeded and minced, or 1 teaspoon ground Asian chili paste*
Available in Asian or gourmet markets.

Combine all ingredients in a nonreactive saucepan over medium heat. Bring to a boil. Lower heat and simmer for 5 minutes. Remove from heat and place in a nonreactive bowl to cool. If too thick, thin with hot water. Serve at room temperature.

PICKLED SHRIMP

SERVES 6 TO 8.

2 bay leaves
1 dried red chili pepper
1 orange, quartered
2 pounds medium shrimp, peeled and deveined
1 large red onion, peeled and finely diced
1 cup fresh orange juice
1 cup fresh lime juice
1 tablespoon extra-virgin olive oil
1 tablespoon minced shallots
1 clove garlic, peeled and minced
1 jalapeño chili pepper (or to taste), seeded and minced
Salt to taste

Place bay leaves, chili, and orange quarters in a large pot of cold water. Bring to a boil. Add shrimp and cook for about 2 minutes or until just opaque. Drain and refresh under cold water. Pat dry.

Combine the cooked shrimp with the remaining ingredients in a nonreactive bowl. Cover and refrigerate for at least 1 hour before serving.

Pickled Shrimp marinating in a canning jar.

NEW YORK PARTIES SHRIMP DIJON

SERVES 6 TO 8.

⅓ cup Dijon-style mustard
2 tablespoons chopped shallots
1 tablespoon chopped fresh Italian parsley
1 tablespoon white-wine vinegar
1 tablespoon red-wine vinegar
¼ cup extra-virgin olive oil
Pinch of red pepper flakes
¾ pound shrimp, cooked, peeled, and deveined

In a food processor fitted with the metal blade, mix together the mustard, shallots, parsley, vinegars, oil, and red pepper flakes. When well blended, pour over the shrimp in a nonreactive container. Cover and refrigerate for at least 2 hours before serving.

SHRIMP TIMBALES WITH FRESH GINGER SAUCE

SERVES 6.

1 pound plus 6 whole, small shrimp, peeled
 and deveined
1 cup heavy cream
1 large egg
½ cup diced yellow bell peppers, blanched
1 tablespoon minced shallots
½ teaspoon minced fresh tarragon
 Dash of Tabasco sauce
 Salt to taste
 Pepper to taste
 Fresh Ginger Sauce
6 sprigs fresh mint

Preheat oven to 350°F.

Spray 6 individual ½-cup molds with nonstick spray. Lay 1 shrimp in the center bottom of each. Place the remaining shrimp in a food processor fitted with the metal blade. Coarsely chop, using quick on-and-off turns. Add cream and egg and process until smooth. Scrape shrimp mixture into a mixing bowl. Stir in peppers, shallots, tarragon, Tabasco, salt, and pepper. When well combined, scrape equal portions into the prepared molds. Place the molds in a shallow baking dish with enough water to come to the halfway mark on the molds. Cover the tops of the molds with buttered foil or parchment paper circles. Place the entire pan in the oven and bake for 15 minutes or until a wooden toothpick inserted in the center of a mold comes out clean. Remove from oven.

Peel off foil covers and invert onto a serving platter or 6 individual serving plates. Allow to set for a couple of minutes. Carefully blot up excess liquid with a paper towel. Spoon Fresh Ginger Sauce around timbales and garnish with mint sprigs.

FRESH GINGER SAUCE

MAKES ABOUT 1 CUP.

1 cup peeled, chopped fresh ginger
⅔ cup sugar
1½ cups water
2 cups champagne
½ cup honeydew puree
⅓ cup chilled unsalted butter
2 teaspoons fresh lime juice
Salt to taste
White pepper to taste

Combine ginger, sugar, and water in a medium saucepan over high heat. Bring to a boil. When boiling, lower heat and simmer for about 40 minutes or until liquid is reduced to ½ cup. Add champagne. Raise heat and again bring to a boil. When boiling, lower heat and simmer for another 30 minutes or until liquid is reduced to ½ cup. Remove from heat and strain through a fine sieve or cheesecloth. Return to the pan. Stir in melon puree. Place over medium heat and bring to just a simmer. When simmering, lower heat and whisk in butter, a bit at a time. When butter is well incorporated, whisk in lime juice, salt, and pepper. Keep warm over hot water until ready to serve.

SPICY SHRIMP PANCAKES WITH CHILI SAUCE

SERVES 6.

¼ pound peeled, deveined, and cooked
    shrimp
2 tablespoons minced shallots
1 tablespoon chopped fresh chives
1 teaspoon minced serrano chili peppers
    (or to taste)
⅓ cup well-drained, chopped, cooked spinach
2 large eggs
⅓ cup all-purpose flour
1 teaspoon baking powder
2 tablespoons nonfat unflavored yogurt
2 teaspoons canola oil
    Salt to taste
    Pepper to taste
    Chili Sauce
6 chive blossoms

Place shrimp, shallots, chives, and chilies in a food processor fitted with the metal blade. Coarsely chop, using quick on-and-off turns. Add spinach, eggs, flour, baking powder, yogurt, oil, salt, and pepper, and process until just mixed. Scrape from bowl and allow to sit for 10 minutes.

Heat a nonstick griddle over medium-high heat. Lightly grease, if necessary. When hot, spoon the shrimp batter onto the griddle to make circles about 3 inches in diameter. Cook for about 3 minutes per side or until lightly browned and set. Continue making pancakes, keeping cooked pancakes warm as you go.

Place about 2 tablespoons Chili Sauce on each of 6 small serving plates. Overlap 3 pancakes down the center and drizzle a bit of sauce on top. Garnish each with a chive blossom.

SHRIMP CANAPES

MAKES 36.

CHILI SAUCE

MAKES ABOUT 2 CUPS.

3 cups fish stock (see page 12) or clam broth
2 cloves garlic, peeled
3 shallots, peeled
1 serrano chili pepper, seeded
1 tablespoon brandy
3 bell peppers, roasted, cored, and seeded
1 tablespoon fresh lime juice
   Salt to taste
   Pepper to taste
3 tablespoons chilled unsalted butter

Place fish stock or clam broth, garlic, shallots, and chili in a small saucepan over medium heat. Bring to a boil. When boiling, lower heat and simmer for 20 minutes or until liquid is reduced to 1 cup. Add brandy and cook for 1 minute. Scrape into the bowl of a food processor fitted with the metal blade. Add bell peppers, lime juice, salt, and pepper. Process until smooth. Return to saucepan over medium heat. When mixture begins to simmer, lower heat and whisk in butter a bit at a time. When butter is well incorporated, remove sauce from heat and keep warm over hot water until ready to use.

3 ounces cream cheese, softened
½ cup mayonnaise
¼ pound cooked shrimp, peeled, deveined, and chopped
2 tablespoons chopped mango chutney
2 tablespoons minced scallions
1 tablespoon chopped toasted almonds
1 teaspoon fresh lemon juice
   Cayenne pepper to taste
36 white toast rounds
   (1½ inches in diameter)

Beat cream cheese and mayonnaise until well blended. Add shrimp, chutney, scallions, almonds, lemon juice, and cayenne.

Preheat broiler.

Spread approximately 1 tablespoon of the shrimp mixture on each toast round, mounding slightly in the center. Place on a broiler tray and broil for about 3 minutes or until the canapés are golden. Serve hot.

SHRIMP TOAST

SERVES 6 TO 8.

1 pound large shrimp, peeled
10 water chestnuts
1 shallot, peeled
1 piece (1 inch) fresh ginger, peeled
1 large egg white, lightly beaten
2 tablespoons cornstarch
1 tablespoon rice wine*
Cayenne pepper to taste
Salt to taste
8 slices stale, homemade-type white bread
¼ cup sesame seeds
About 4 cups vegetable oil

Available in Asian or gourmet markets.

Place shrimp, water chestnuts, shallot, and ginger in a food processor fitted with the metal blade. Mince, using quick on-and-off turns and being careful not to puree. When minced, place in a small mixing bowl and lightly stir in egg white, cornstarch, wine, cayenne, and salt. Do not overmix.

Trim the crust from the bread and cut each slice into four triangles. Generously coat each triangle with the shrimp mixture, mounding slightly in the center and carefully smoothing the edges. Sprinkle each triangle with sesame seeds, gently pushing the seeds into the shrimp mixture.

Heat the oil in a wok over medium-high heat until it reaches 375°F on a food thermometer. When oil is hot, use tongs to lower the shrimp triangles into the oil, shrimp side down. When the edges begin to brown, turn and fry the other side. When golden, remove and drain on paper towels. Keep warm until ready to serve.

BROCHETTES OF SHRIMP AND PAPAYA

SERVES 6.

¾ cup peanut oil
  Juice of 2 limes
2 tablespoons fresh orange juice
1 tablespoon maple syrup
2 teaspoons sake*
2 cloves garlic, peeled and minced
1 teaspoon grated fresh ginger
1 teaspoon minced fresh mint
  Salt to taste
  Pepper to taste
18 large shrimp, peeled and deveined
1 large, firm, ripe papaya
6 lemon slices
6 orange slices

Available in Asian or gourmet markets.

Soak 6 bamboo skewers in cold water.

Combine oil, citrus juices, syrup, sake, garlic, ginger, mint, salt and pepper. Place shrimp in a nonreactive shallow dish. Peel and seed papaya and cut into 12 1-inch cubes. Add to shrimp. Pour marinade over the shrimp and papaya. Cover and refrigerate for 1 hour.

Preheat grill or broiler.

Thread 3 shrimp and 2 papaya cubes alternately onto each wet bamboo skewer. Place on the grill or under the broiler for about 4 minutes or until the shrimp are just firm and the papaya is glazed.

Place 1 skewer on each of 6 small serving plates. Drizzle each brochette with remaining marinade and garnish each plate with a lemon and orange slice.

CHAPTER II

Hot and Cold Soups

These soups are some of my favorites, but it really is quite simple to revise your own favorites to feature shrimp. Almost any soup usually made with fish or chicken can be made using shrimp alone or in combination with the standard item. The only rule to remember is that shrimp cannot withstand long periods of cooking. So unlike traditional back-of-the-stove simmering soup pots, any shrimp soup should have the flavor simmered, with the shrimp added just at the end of cooking.

SIMPLE SHRIMP CHOWDER

SERVES 6.

1 tablespoon vegetable oil
½ cup diced shallots
2 tablespoons minced celery
2 tablespoons minced fresh parsley
1 clove garlic, peeled and minced
1½ cups diced baking potatoes
1 cup diced carrots
½ cup diced red bell peppers
2 cups fish stock (see page 12)
2 cups unsalted, defatted chicken stock
1 teaspoon minced fresh dill
½ teaspoon minced fresh thyme
Salt to taste
Pepper to taste
1 cup chopped canned plum tomatoes
1½ pounds medium shrimp, peeled and deveined
½ cup heavy cream (optional)

Heat oil in a heavy sauté pan over medium-high heat. When hot, add shallots, celery, parsley, and garlic. Sauté, stirring constantly, for about 3 minutes or until vegetables are soft. Stir in potatoes, carrots, and peppers. Add stocks, herbs, salt, and pepper. Bring to a boil. Add tomatoes and again bring to a boil. When boiling, lower heat and simmer for 10 minutes. Stir in shrimp and again bring to a boil. Lower heat. Cover and simmer for 6 minutes. Stir in cream, if desired, and serve immediately.

SPINACH AND SHRIMP SOUP

SERVES 6.

2 cups fish stock (see page 12)
2 cups unsalted, defatted chicken stock
1 cup water
1 tablespoon minced garlic
2 tablespoons light soy sauce
1 pound medium shrimp, cooked, peeled, deveined, and halved lengthwise
¾ pound spinach leaves, washed, dried, and shredded
½ cup sliced scallions
¼ cup diced Virginia ham
Pepper to taste
2 tablespoons toasted sesame seeds

Place stocks, water, garlic, and soy sauce in a large saucepan over high heat. Bring to a boil and boil for 5 minutes. Remove from heat and stir in shrimp, spinach, scallions, ham, and pepper. Taste and adjust seasoning with soy sauce and pepper, if necessary. Serve immediately, sprinkled with sesame seeds.

Simple Shrimp Chowder garnished with a sprig of fresh dill.

CRUNCHY BUTTERMILK SHRIMP SOUP

SERVES 6.

¾ **pound shrimp, peeled and deveined**
1 **tablespoon olive oil**
1 **teaspoon Tabasco sauce**
  Juice of 1 lemon
2 **cups buttermilk**
1½ **cups heavy cream**
½ **cup nonfat unflavored yogurt**
2 **tablespoons fruit-flavored vinegar (such as raspberry)**
¼ **cup minced fresh cilantro**
1 **tablespoon minced fresh mint**
1 **tablespoon frozen apple juice concentrate**
  Salt to taste
  Pepper to taste
½ **cup finely diced raw artichoke hearts**
½ **cup finely diced jícama***
½ **cup finely diced yellow bell peppers**
½ **cup finely diced green bell peppers**
¼ **cup shredded basil leaves**

*Available in Latin American and many fine produce markets.

Combine shrimp, oil, Tabasco, and lemon juice, tossing to coat the shrimp. Place in a nonstick sauté pan over medium heat. Sauté for about 3 minutes or until shrimp have curled and are just pink. Remove from heat and drain on paper towels.

Place buttermilk, cream, yogurt, vinegar, cilantro, and mint in a blender. Process until smooth. Add the juice concentrate, salt, and pepper, and process until well combined.

Pour buttermilk mixture into a serving bowl. Chop shrimp and add to buttermilk with remaining vegetables and basil. Cover and refrigerate for 1 hour. Taste and adjust seasoning with salt, pepper, and lime juice, if necessary. Serve cold.

SHRIMP MINESTRONE

SERVES 6 TO 8.

¼ cup extra-virgin olive oil
¼ cup unsalted butter or margarine
1 cup chopped onions
1 cup chopped leeks
¼ cup minced fresh Italian parsley
1 teaspoon minced fresh thyme
2 cups diced potatoes
2 cups diced carrots
1 cup diced celery
1 cup diced zucchini
1 cup fresh fava beans
1 cup fresh or frozen green peas
2 cups canned Italian plum tomatoes (with juice)
4 cups shrimp or fish stock (see page 12)
2 cups vegetable stock
Salt to taste
Pepper to taste
1 pound shrimp, peeled, deveined, and chopped
2 tablespoons shredded fresh basil
¼ cup freshly grated Parmesan cheese

Heat oil and butter or margarine in a large stock pot over medium-high heat. When hot, stir in onions, leeks, parsley, and thyme. Lower heat and sauté for about 5 minutes or until onions begin to brown. Add remaining vegetables (except tomatoes), one at a time, sautéing each for about 3 minutes. When all the vegetables are sautéed, stir in tomatoes, stocks, salt, and pepper. Raise heat and bring to a boil. When boiling, lower heat to a simmer and continue to simmer, for about 1 hour, until soup is quite thick. Add shrimp and continue to cook for about 5 minutes. Remove from heat. Stir in basil. Ladle into soup bowls and sprinkle with Parmesan. Serve immediately.

SHRIMP GAZPACHO

SERVES 6.

6 large, very ripe tomatoes, peeled, cored, and seeded

2 large cucumbers, peeled and seeded

2 cloves garlic, peeled

1 serrano chili pepper (or to taste), cored and seeded

1½ cups unsalted vegetable or clam broth, V-8, Clamato, or tomato juice

¼ cup extra-virgin olive oil

¼ cup red-wine vinegar

Juice of 1 lime

1 red bell pepper

1 green bell pepper

1 bunch scallions, washed and trimmed

1 stalk celery, washed and trimmed

¾ pound shrimp, cooked, peeled, deveined, and chopped

Salt to taste

Pepper to taste

2 tablespoons minced fresh cilantro

1 tablespoon minced fresh mint

6 tablespoons nonfat unflavored yogurt or sour cream (optional)

Coarsely chop tomatoes and 1 cucumber. Place chopped vegetables, garlic, chili, vegetable or clam broth, oil, vinegar, and lime juice in a blender. Process until very smooth. Pour tomato mixture into a nonreactive container.

Wash bell peppers. Core, seed, and finely dice. Add to tomato mixture. Finely dice remaining cucumber and add to tomato mixture. Cut scallions into fine slices and add to tomato mixture. Finely dice celery and add to tomato mixture. Stir shrimp into soup. Add salt and pepper. Cover and refrigerate for 1 hour to allow flavors to blend. Taste and adjust seasoning with salt and pepper and extra lime juice, if necessary. Stir in cilantro and mint. Serve cold with a dollop of yogurt or sour cream, if desired.

Shrimp Gazpacho garnished with sour cream and lime wedges.

LEMON GRASS AND SHRIMP SOUP WITH RED CURRY

SERVES 6 TO 8.

6 stalks fresh lemon grass*

8 cups water

¼ cup minced shallots

1½ cups canned straw mushrooms*, well drained

¼ cup fish sauce (such as nuoc nam or nam pla)*

¼ cup Red Curry (optional)

1½ pounds medium shrimp, peeled and deveined

2 kaffir lime leaves (makrut leaves)*

3 small dried red chili peppers

2 tablespoons fresh lime juice

¼ cup cilantro leaves

Available in Asian or gourmet markets.

Trim the lemon grass to yield only the tenderest 6 inches of the bottom. Slice each stalk in half lengthwise and pound slightly.

Pour water into a wok over high heat. Add the lemon grass, shallots, mushrooms, fish sauce, and Red Curry (if using). Boil for 5 minutes.

Add the shrimp and cook only until shrimp turn pink. Immediately add kaffir lime leaves, chilies, and lime juice. Cover and let stand 3 minutes.

Pour into individual serving bowls or into a soup tureen and sprinkle cilantro on top.

RED CURRY

MAKES ABOUT ½ CUP.

10 dried red chili peppers, stemmed

2 pieces galangal*

1 teaspoon kaffir lime rind (makrut rind)*

1 teaspoon caraway seeds

1 teaspoon coriander seeds

3 tablespoons minced lemon grass*

3 tablespoons minced garlic

2 tablespoons minced cilantro stems

10 black peppercorns

¼ teaspoon ground cinnamon

1 tablespoon minced fresh ginger

½ teaspoon ground turmeric

1 tablespoon shrimp paste*

Available in Asian or gourmet markets.

Soak the chilies, galangal, and kaffir lime rind in 1 cup hot water for 15 minutes or until soft. When soft, drain well and chop into small pieces.

Place caraway and coriander seeds in a small frying pan. Dry-fry them over medium heat for about 3 minutes or until browned and aromatic.

Combine all ingredients and grind to a smooth paste using a mortar and pestle or a blender. If using a blender, you may have to add a bit of water or vegetable oil to facilitate processing.

When well blended, place in a covered container and refrigerate until ready to use.

Red Curry will keep, covered and refrigerated, for 1 month.

SHRIMP AND LENTIL SOUP

SERVES 6 TO 8.

1 cup dried lentils
½ cup diced yellow onions
2 cloves garlic, peeled and minced
3 cups water
1 cup fish stock (see page 12) or clam broth
  Salt to taste
1 teaspoon ground cumin
½ teaspoon ground coriander
¼ teaspoon curry powder
¼ teaspoon cayenne pepper (or to taste)
1 tablespoon fresh lime juice
1 pound small shrimp, peeled and deveined
1 cup peeled, seeded, and diced tomatoes
¼ cup finely diced red onions
¼ cup chopped cilantro leaves
¼ cup sour cream or nonflavored yogurt (optional)

Place lentils, yellow onions, garlic, and water in a deep saucepan over high heat. Bring to a boil. When boiling, lower heat, cover, and simmer for about 30 minutes or until lentils have become a thick puree, adding additional water, if necessary. Add fish stock or clam broth, salt, spices, and lime juice and cook for 10 minutes. Stir in shrimp, tomatoes, and red onions and cook for 3 minutes or until the shrimp are just pink. Stir in cilantro and serve the soup immediately with a dollop of sour cream or yogurt on top, if desired.

SHRIMP BISQUE

SERVES 6.

2 pounds shrimp

2 cups fish stock (see page 12)

1 cup milk

1 cup finely diced celery

¼ cup finely diced onions

2 tablespoons unsalted butter

2 tablespoons all-purpose flour

¼ cup peeled, seeded, and finely diced tomatoes

2 cups heavy cream

1 tablespoon sherry

Paprika to taste

Salt to taste

Pepper to taste

Place shrimp and fish stock in a heavy saucepan over high heat. Bring to a boil. When boiling, lower heat and simmer for 3 minutes. Drain, reserving liquid.

Peel, devein, and chop shrimp. Set aside.

Return reserved liquid to the saucepan. Add milk, celery, and onions, and bring to a boil over high heat. Cover. Lower heat and simmer for 5 minutes. Remove from heat.

Melt butter in a medium saucepan over medium heat. When melted, add flour and stir to incorporate. When well incorporated, whisk in fish stock until smooth. Add tomatoes and cream. Raise heat and bring to a boil. Immediately lower heat and simmer for about 5 minutes or until slightly thickened. Whisk in sherry and paprika until well blended. Add shrimp, salt, and pepper. Serve hot.

JELLIED SHRIMP MADRILENE

SERVES 6.

3 cups unsalted, defatted chicken stock

2 cups fish stock (see page 12) or clam broth

1 cup tomato puree

2 tablespoons Madeira

¾ cup minced red onions

1 clove garlic, peeled and chopped

3 tablespoons minced fresh parsley

1 teaspoon minced fresh thyme

1 teaspoon minced fresh lemon sage

1 teaspoon minced fresh chives

2 egg shells, broken into pieces

2 egg whites, slightly beaten

Salt to taste

White pepper to taste

2 envelopes unflavored gelatin

½ cup cold water

18 large cooked shrimp, peeled and deveined

2 tablespoons minced pickled ginger* or 2 tablespoons prepared horseradish, well drained (optional)

6 lemon wedges

Available in Asian or gourmet markets.

Combine stocks, tomato puree, Madeira, onions, garlic, herbs, egg shells, egg whites, salt, and pepper in a medium nonreactive saucepan over medium-high heat. Bring to a boil and allow to boil for 10 minutes. Remove from heat.

To make consommé, dissolve gelatin in the water. When dissolved, whisk into the flavored broth and allow to stand for 8 minutes. Strain through a fine sieve or through cheesecloth into a 2-quart container. Cover and refrigerate until firm.

Chop 6 shrimp and place equal portions into each of 6 individual soup cups. Cut chilled consommè into small cubes and place over chopped shrimp. Garnish tops with pickled ginger or horseradish, if desired. Place two shrimp opposite each other on the edges of each soup cup and place a lemon wedge on the side of each cup. Serve immediately or cover and refrigerate until ready to serve.

COLD AVOCADO AND SHRIMP SOUP

SERVES 6.

2 large, ripe avocados, peeled, seeded, and
  chopped
Juice of 2 lemons
¼ bunch watercress, washed and dried
3 scallions, washed and trimmed
2 cups fish stock (see page 12) or clam broth
1 cup milk
1½ pounds cooked, peeled, and deveined
  shrimp
Tabasco sauce to taste
Salt to taste
Pepper to taste
2 cups heavy cream
2 tablespoons chopped fresh chives

Place avocado in a blender with lemon juice, watercress, scallions, fish stock or clam broth, and milk. Process until pureed. Add half the shrimp and again process until smooth. Season with Tabasco, salt, and pepper, and blend to mix. Pour into a nonreactive container. Chop remaining shrimp and add to soup along with cream. Stir to blend. Cover and refrigerate for 1 hour before serving. Garnish with chives.

**Cold Avocado and Shrimp Soup garnished with
whole poached shrimp, a lemon slice, and chive stalks.**

SHRIMP SOUP WITH AVGOLEMONO SAUCE

SERVES 6.

3½ cups fish stock (see page 12)
3½ cups unsalted, defatted chicken stock
1 cup diced fresh fennel
1 cup diced red bell peppers
1 leek, white part only, diced
1 cup cooked orzo or rice
1 pound small shrimp, peeled and deveined
Salt to taste
Pepper to taste
4 large eggs
Juice of 2 lemons

Place stocks in a heavy saucepan over high heat. Bring to a boil. Add fennel, peppers, and leek, and again bring to a boil. When boiling, lower heat and simmer for 5 minutes. Stir in orzo or rice, shrimp, salt, and pepper, and cook about 3 minutes or until shrimp are just tender.

Beat eggs well. When well beaten, whisk in lemon juice. Gradually whisk about 1 cup of the hot soup stock into the egg mixture to warm the eggs. Slowly whisk the egg mixture into the hot soup. Bring the soup to a simmer, stirring constantly. Do not boil. Serve immediately.

CHAPTER III

Sensational Salads

Throughout this section, feel free to replace the style of cooked shrimp directed in the recipe with any other type. For instance, if it is easier to grill shrimp, do so instead of simply boiling them.

If you have a favorite salad that normally would not call for shrimp, try replacing the meat or poultry with the ubiquitous shrimp. Infrequently, you might have to adjust some of the seasonings, but this will not usually be necessary.

GREEK SHRIMP SALAD

SERVES 6.

½ cup Greek olive oil

2 pounds medium shrimp, peeled and deveined

Juice of 2 lemons

1 clove garlic, peeled and minced

1 tablespoon minced fresh oregano

2 teaspoons minced fresh mint

Salt to taste

Pepper to taste

¼ pound feta cheese, crumbled

4 plum tomatoes, cut into wedges

¼ cup chopped scallions

1 head chicory, washed, dried, and pulled apart

½ cup Calamata olives, pitted

2 tablespoons minced fresh parsley

Place 1 tablespoon oil in heavy sauté pan over medium-high heat. When hot, add shrimp and sauté for about 3 minutes or until shrimp are just firm. Remove pan from heat.

Place shrimp in a bowl and add remaining oil to sauté pan. Return pan to heat. Whisk in lemon juice, garlic, oregano, mint, salt, and pepper. When well blended, remove from heat and pour over shrimp. Allow shrimp to cool.

When cool, toss in feta, tomatoes, and scallions. Place chicory on a serving platter. Pour the shrimp over it. Sprinkle with olives and parsley and serve immediately.

WARM SHRIMP SALAD

SERVES 6.

8 cups California spinach leaves, washed and dried

2 cups sliced, cooked potatoes (preferably Peruvian Purple or Yellow Finn)

1 red onion, peeled and sliced

1 tablespoon olive oil

1½ pounds medium shrimp, peeled and deveined

1 tablespoon fresh lemon juice

1 tablespoon fresh orange juice

2 tablespoons prepared honey mustard

Salt to taste

Pepper to taste

¼ cup chopped scallions

Combine the spinach, potatoes, and onion slices. Place on a serving platter.

Heat oil in a sauté pan. When hot, add shrimp and sauté for 2 to 3 minutes or until just firm. Remove from heat and stir in citrus juices and honey mustard. Add salt and pepper.

Place the warm shrimp down the center of the spinach mixture. Sprinkle with scallions and serve immediately.

Greek Shrimp Salad served with warm pita bread.

SHRIMP IN TOMATO DRESSING

SERVES 6.

1½ pounds large cooked, peeled, and deveined shrimp

4 very ripe plum tomatoes, peeled, cored, and seeded

8 cloves garlic, roasted (see Note)

½ cup heavy cream

1 cup mayonnaise

3 tablespoons fresh lemon juice

Salt to taste

Pepper to taste

2 bunches watercress, washed, trimmed, and dried

½ cup seeded, diced tomatoes

Place shrimp in a bowl. Process plum tomatoes, garlic, cream, mayonnaise, lemon juice, salt, and pepper in a food processor fitted with the metal blade. When smooth, pour over the shrimp.

Place watercress on a serving platter. Place shrimp in the center and sprinkle with the diced tomatoes. Serve immediately.

Note: To roast garlic, first lightly rub unpeeled cloves with olive oil and then place in a preheated 350°F oven for 15 minutes or until garlic pulp is soft. Remove skin before using.

RUBIE'S CAROLINA SHRIMP SALAD

SERVES 6.

1½ pounds large cooked, peeled, and deveined shrimp

2 red onions, peeled and sliced

1 green bell pepper, cored, seeded, and diced

3 stalks celery, washed, trimmed, and sliced

½ cup canola oil

¼ cup ketchup

1 tablespoon molasses

2 teaspoons Worcestershire sauce

½ teaspoon dry mustard

½ teaspoon hot-pepper sauce

¼ teaspoon ground thyme

2 bay leaves

Salt to taste

Pepper to taste

1 head iceberg lettuce, washed and shredded

2 tomatoes, peeled, cored, and cut into wedges

Place shrimp, onions, peppers, and celery in a nonreactive container. Combine oil, ketchup, molasses, Worcestershire sauce, mustard, hot-pepper sauce, thyme, bay leaves, salt, and pepper. Pour over shrimp. Cover and refrigerate for at least 6 hours.

When ready to serve, line a platter with lettuce. Remove the shrimp from the refrigerator. Discard bay leaves and pour shrimp with marinade over the lettuce. Garnish with tomatoes.

SHRIMP CAESAR SALAD

SERVES 6.

Salt
1 clove garlic, peeled
2 medium heads romaine lettuce
1 can (2 ounces) anchovies, well drained and chopped
¼ cup olive oil
1 tablespoon fresh lemon juice
¼ cup freshly grated Parmesan cheese
1 large egg, softly boiled
1 cup freshly made French bread croutons
24 grilled jumbo shrimp, warm

Sprinkle salt in a wooden bowl. Rub salt into the bowl with the garlic clove until salt is moist and well flavored.

Remove any damaged leaves and pull romaine heads apart. Wash and dry well. Break leaves into pieces and place in the seasoned bowl. Toss anchovies into romaine. Add individually the oil, lemon juice, Parmesan, egg, and croutons, tossing to coat after each addition.

Place equal portions of the salad on 6 warm serving plates. Place 4 shrimp on top of each portion and serve immediately.

SHRIMP RÉMOULADE

SERVES 6.

1 pound large cooked, peeled, and deveined shrimp
1 avocado, peeled, seeded, and diced
1 celery root, peeled and julienned
1½ cups Rémoulade Sauce (see page 121)
1 head red-leaf lettuce and/or radicchio, pulled apart, washed, and dried
½ cup peeled, seeded, and diced tomatoes

Combine shrimp, avocado, celery root, and Rémoulade Sauce. Make a cup of lettuce or radicchio on each of 6 chilled plates. Place a mound of Shrimp Rémoulade in the center of the lettuce. Sprinkle with tomatoes and serve immediately.

THAI SHRIMP AND PEANUT SALAD

SERVES 6.

½ cup raspberry vinegar

½ cup soy sauce

¼ cup smooth peanut butter

¼ cup black bean sauce*

1 tablespoon Japanese sweet rice wine*

1 serrano chili pepper (or to taste), seeded and minced

3 tablespoons minced fresh ginger

1 clove garlic, peeled and minced

1 teaspoon brown sugar

½ cup peanut oil

1 teaspoon sesame oil

Salt to taste

Pepper to taste

½ cup chopped cilantro leaves

1 pound thin (number 9) spaghetti, cooked and well drained

1½ pounds large cooked shrimp, peeled and deveined

1½ cups roasted unsalted peanuts

½ cup chopped scallions

1 bunch watercress, washed and dried (optional)

Available in Asian or gourmet markets.

Combine vinegar, soy sauce, peanut butter, bean sauce, wine, chilies, ginger, garlic, and brown sugar. Stir until sugar is dissolved. Whisk in oils, salt, and pepper. When well combined, stir in about half of the cilantro.

Place spaghetti in a large bowl and pour dressing on top. Toss in the shrimp, 1 cup peanuts, scallions, and remaining cilantro and combine. When well combined, mound on a serving platter and sprinkle with remaining peanuts. Garnish platter with watercress, if desired.

Thai Shrimp and Peanut Salad garnished with watercress and cucumber.

BLACK BEAN AND SHRIMP SALAD

SERVES 6.

1½ pounds large cooked, peeled, and
 deveined shrimp

2 cups cooked black beans, well drained

1 cup diced jícama*

1 cup cooked corn kernels

1 medium red bell pepper, cored, seeded,
 and diced

1 medium green bell pepper, cored, seeded,
 and diced

½ cup diced red onions

1 cup tightly packed cilantro leaves

1 bunch scallions, white parts only

1 clove garlic, peeled

1 serrano chili pepper (or to taste), cored
 and seeded

1 cup fresh lime juice

¼ cup fresh orange juice

¼ cup olive oil

1 teaspoon maple syrup (or to taste)
 Salt to taste
 Pepper to taste

¼ cup peanut oil

6 corn tortillas

2 cups chopped lettuce

12 slices avocado

*Available in Latin American and many fine
 produce markets.

Reserve 12 whole shrimp. Chop remaining shrimp and combine with black beans, jícama, corn, peppers, and onions in a nonreactive bowl. Place cilantro, scallions, garlic, chili, lime juice, 2 tablespoons orange juice, olive oil, syrup, salt, and pepper in a blender. Process until smooth. When smooth, pour over shrimp mixture and toss to combine. Cover and refrigerate for 1 hour.

Heat the peanut oil in a heavy skillet over medium heat. When hot, fry the tortillas, one at a time, until crisp. Drain the tortillas on paper towels.

Place 1 tortilla on each of 6 serving plates. Sprinkle with chopped lettuce. Top with equal portions of shrimp mixture. Sprinkle remaining orange juice on avocado slices. Place an avocado slice and 1 whole shrimp on opposite sides of each tortilla. Serve immediately.

Black Bean and Shrimp Salad
garnished with whole poached shrimp, avocado slices, and lime.

SHRIMP AND TOMATO ASPIC WITH SPICY CREAM CHEESE

SERVES 6 TO 8.

2½ cups peeled, seeded, and chopped very ripe or canned, well-drained tomatoes
1 cup diced onions
1 clove garlic, peeled and minced
3 peppercorns
4 whole cloves
1 bay leaf
½ teaspoon paprika
¼ teaspoon cayenne pepper (or to taste)
2 tablespoons sugar
1 teaspoon salt (or to taste)
2 envelopes unflavored gelatin
½ cup cold water
1 tablespoon fresh lemon juice
1 cup cubed avocado
½ cup diced yellow bell peppers
½ cup diced red bell peppers
½ cup diced red onions
1½ pounds small cooked shrimp, peeled and deveined
Lettuce or watercress (optional)
Spicy Cream Cheese

Combine tomatoes, onions, garlic, peppercorns, cloves, bay leaf, paprika, cayenne, sugar, and salt in a medium, nonreactive saucepan over medium-high heat. Cover and bring to a boil. When boiling, lower heat and simmer for about 15 minutes or until vegetables are soft. Remove from heat and strain through a fine sieve or cheesecloth into a bowl.

Measure 2½ cups of liquid. Place in a clean saucepan and bring to a boil over high heat. When boiling, turn off heat and let the liquid stand.

To make aspic, soften gelatin in the water. When softened, whisk into strained tomato mixture along with lemon juice. Taste and adjust seasoning, if necessary. Refrigerate for about 1 hour, until gelatin begins to thicken. When mixture begins to congeal, stir in avocado, peppers, red onions, and shrimp.

Rinse a 4-cup mold in very cold water (or very lightly coat with vegetable oil). Immediately pour in tomato mixture. Cover with clear plastic wrap and refrigerate until firm.

To serve, line a cold platter with lettuce or watercress, if desired. Unmold tomato aspic by either quickly dipping the mold into very hot water or wrapping it in a hot, wet towel for a few seconds, and inverting it into the center of the platter. Pipe rosettes of Spicy Cream Cheese around the edges and serve immediately. Or unmold and decorate, and immediately refrigerate until ready to serve.

SHRIMP LOUIS

SERVES 6 TO 8.

2 cups mayonnaise
¼ cup buttermilk
2 tablespoons white vinegar
¾ cup bottled cocktail sauce
¼ cup grated onions
  Tabasco sauce to taste
  Lemon juice to taste
1 large head iceberg lettuce
1½ pounds cooked jumbo shrimp, peeled and deveined
2 ripe tomatoes, peeled, cored, and cut into wedges
2 hard-boiled eggs, peeled and cut into quarters
1 tablespoon capers, well drained

Combine mayonnaise, buttermilk, vinegar, cocktail sauce, onions, Tabasco, and lemon juice. Set aside.

Peel off outer leaves of lettuce. Wash and dry well.

Line a serving platter or salad bowl with whole lettuce leaves. Wash and dry remaining lettuce. Chop coarsely and line platter or bowl to make a salad bed. Pour the mayonnaise mixture over lettuce. Place shrimp, tomatoes, and eggs decoratively over the top. Sprinkle with capers and serve immediately.

SPICY CREAM CHEESE

MAKES ½ CUP.

1 package (4 ounces) cream cheese
1 teaspoon Dijon-style mustard
1 teaspoon Tabasco sauce (or to taste)
  Dash cayenne pepper

Beat all the ingredients together until well blended. Scrape into a pastry bag fitted with the rosette tube. Refrigerate until ready to use.

SEAFOOD CHEF'S SALAD

SERVES 6 TO 8.

6 to 8 cups mixed field greens
1 pound shrimp, peeled, deveined, and grilled
½ pound tuna steak, grilled and cut into chunks
½ pound cooked lobster or crabmeat
2 hard-boiled eggs, peeled and quartered
2 tomatoes, peeled and cut into wedges
1 red bell pepper, roasted, seeded, and cut into strips
¾ cup extra-virgin olive oil
¼ cup raspberry vinegar
1 teaspoon balsamic vinegar
1 tablespoon finely chopped mixed herbs
1 clove garlic, peeled and minced
Salt to taste
Pepper to taste
½ cup crumbled goat cheese

Place greens in a large shallow salad bowl. Place shrimp in the center. Place tuna and lobster or crabmeat on opposite sides of the bowl. Place equal portions of eggs, tomatoes, and red peppers opposite each other. Whisk together the oil, vinegars, herbs, garlic, salt, and pepper. Pour over salad. Sprinkle with cheese. At the table, toss all ingredients together and serve immediately.

Seafood Chef's Salad.

ITALIAN SEAFOOD SALAD

SERVES 6 TO 8.

1½ pounds medium shrimp, cooked, peeled, and deveined
1 pound cooked squid, sliced
1½ pounds cooked fresh mussels, shelled
1 pound cooked lobster or crabmeat
1½ cups extra-virgin olive oil
½ cup fresh lemon juice
3 tablespoons minced garlic
2 tablespoons minced fresh parsley
1 tablespoon minced fresh basil
½ teaspoon red pepper flakes
Salt to taste
Pepper to taste
2 cups sliced celery
1 cup diced onions

Toss seafood together. Whisk together oil, lemon juice, garlic, herbs, red pepper flakes, salt, and pepper. When blended, pour over the seafood. Cover and refrigerate for 2 hours, stirring frequently.

To serve, stir in celery and onions and serve immediately.

SHRIMP AND COUSCOUS SALAD

SERVES 6 TO 8.

1 tablespoon unsalted butter

2 cups quick-cooking couscous*

1½ pounds shrimp, cooked, peeled, and deveined

1½ cups cooked fresh corn kernels

½ cup diced sweet onions

½ cup diced red bell peppers

¼ cup minced fresh cilantro

¼ cup diced scallions

1 serrano chili pepper (or to taste), seeded and minced

⅔ cup canola oil

Juice of 2 limes

Salt to taste

Pepper to taste

Mixed greens or spinach (optional)

Available in Middle Eastern or gourmet markets.

Bring 3 cups water to a boil in a heavy saucepan over high heat. When boiling, add butter and couscous. Cover and remove from heat. Let stand for 10 minutes. Scrape into a bowl and stir in remaining ingredients except greens or spinach. Cover and refrigerate for about 1 hour to allow flavors to blend. Serve alone or on a bed of greens or spinach, if desired.

Shrimp and Couscous Salad served on a bed of mixed lettuces.

TUSCAN SHRIMP SALAD

SERVES 6 TO 8.

1 cup extra-virgin olive oil

1 loaf crusty Italian country bread, sliced

1½ pounds cooked medium shrimp, peeled and deveined

2 cups cooked white beans, well drained

3 very ripe tomatoes, peeled, cored, and cut into wedges

¼ cup julienned basil leaves

⅓ cup white-wine vinegar

2 cloves garlic, peeled and minced

1 teaspoon sugar

Salt to taste

Pepper to taste

Preheat broiler.

Use ⅓ cup oil to brush both sides of each slice of bread. Place the bread on a broiler tray and grill for about 2 minutes per side or until each side is golden. (Alternatively, use an outdoor grill.)

Combine shrimp, beans, tomatoes, and basil in a nonreactive bowl. Whisk together remaining oil, vinegar, garlic, sugar, salt, and pepper, and pour over shrimp. Cover and allow to marinate for 1 hour.

Line a serving platter with the grilled bread. Pour shrimp salad over the top and serve immediately.

WILD RICE AND SHRIMP SALAD

SERVES 6.

1½ **pounds medium shrimp**
1 **cup white wine**
1 **tablespoon grated orange zest**
1 **teaspoon white peppercorns**
1 **teaspoon coriander seeds**
½ **teaspoon mustard seeds**
1 **bay leaf**
4 **sprigs parsley**
4 **cups cooked wild rice**
1 **cup frozen petit peas, thawed**
1 **cup diced cooked carrots**
1 **tablespoon minced fresh herbs (parsley, tarragon, and dill is a good combination)**
⅓ **cup white-wine vinegar**
1 **tablespoon minced shallots**
1 **teaspoon dry mustard**
⅔ **cup olive oil**
  Salt to taste
  Pepper to taste
  Watercress sprigs

Place shrimp, wine, orange zest, peppercorns, coriander seeds, mustard seeds, bay leaf, and parsley in a saucepan over high heat. Cover and bring to a boil. Remove from heat and allow to sit for about 30 minutes.

Drain shrimp. Peel and devein, then combine with rice, peas, carrots, and herbs. Combine vinegar, shallots, and mustard. Whisk in oil and add salt and pepper. Pour over rice mixture. Cover and refrigerate for at least 2 hours or until just chilled.

Place chilled salad on serving platter. Garnish with watercress and serve immediately.

Sensational Salads

SAUTÉED SHRIMP SALAD WITH TARRAGON BALSAMIC VINAIGRETTE

SERVES 6.

1½ pounds large shrimp, peeled and deveined
1 cup all-purpose flour
1 tablespoon grated lemon zest
Salt to taste
Pepper to taste
3 tablespoons extra-virgin olive oil
3 tablespoons balsamic vinegar
¼ cup white wine
1 tablespoon minced fresh tarragon
¼ cup chilled unsalted butter
6 to 8 cups mixed field greens or 6 hearts of romaine lettuce, washed and dried

Pat shrimp dry. Combine flour, lemon zest, salt, and pepper. Lightly dredge shrimp in flour mixture.

Heat oil in sauté pan over medium heat. When hot, add shrimp, a few at a time, and sauté for about 3 minutes or until just firm and lightly browned. Remove from the pan and keep warm until all the shrimp are sautéed.

Deglaze pan with vinegar. Stir in wine and tarragon and cook for about 5 minutes or until reduced and slightly thickened. Whisk in butter a bit at a time.

Place greens on a serving platter. Place warm shrimp down the center and ladle the warm balsamic vinaigrette over the top. Serve immediately.

SOBA NOODLE SALAD WITH SHRIMP AND PICKLED GINGER

SERVES 6 TO 8.

1 pound soba noodles (also called Japanese buckwheat noodles)*

2 tablespoons vegetable oil

1 cup sliced shiitake mushrooms

1½ pounds cooked small shrimp, peeled and deveined

1 cup bean sprouts

1 cup julienned snow peas

1 cup shredded carrots

¼ cup shredded pickled ginger*

¼ cup light soy sauce

¼ cup unsalted, defatted chicken stock

¼ cup Japanese sweet rice-wine vinegar*

1 tablespoon pickled ginger juice*

1 teaspoon sesame oil*

½ teaspoon chili oil*

1 teaspoon minced fresh ginger

1 clove garlic, peeled and minced

Juice of 1 lime

2 tablespoons black sesame seeds* (optional)

*Available in Asian or gourmet markets.

Cook noodles as directed on package until al dente. Drain. Rinse under cold running water. Drain well. Toss with 1 tablespoon vegetable oil. Set aside.

Heat remaining vegetable oil in heavy sauté pan over medium heat. When hot, add mushrooms. Sauté for 5 minutes. Scrape into noodles. Add shrimp, bean sprouts, peas, carrots, and pickled ginger to noodles and toss to combine.

Whisk together remaining ingredients except sesame seeds. When well combined, pour over noodles and toss to combine. Place on a serving platter and sprinkle with sesame seeds, if desired. Serve immediately.

Soba Noodle Salad with Shrimp and Pickled Ginger.

TOASTED ALMOND SHRIMP SALAD

SERVES 6.

1½ pounds medium shrimp, cooked, peeled and deveined
1 cup seedless green grapes, halved
1 cup toasted slivered almonds
1 stalk celery, washed, trimmed, and finely diced
¾ cup mayonnaise
¼ cup sour cream
1 tablespoon fresh lemon juice
1 tablespoon grated onions
1 teaspoon grated fresh ginger
Bibb or Boston lettuce, pulled apart, washed, and dried
6 slices cooked bacon, crumbled

Combine shrimp, grapes, almonds, and celery. Whisk together mayonnaise, sour cream, lemon juice, onions, and ginger. When well combined, add half of the dressing to the shrimp. Toss to coat the shrimp.

Line a serving platter with lettuce. Place the shrimp salad in the center. Sprinkle with bacon. Serve with the remaining flavored mayonnaise on the side.

SHRIMP AND PENNE SALAD

SERVES 6 TO 8.

1 pound penne
¾ cup olive oil
1½ pounds shrimp, grilled, peeled, and deveined
1 pound ripe plum tomatoes, peeled, seeded, and diced
½ pound mozzarella, diced
½ cup chopped fresh Italian parsley
¼ cup chopped fresh basil
Salt to taste
Pepper to taste

Cook penne in rapidly boiling salted water as directed on package until al dente. When cooked, remove from heat and drain well. Place penne in a bowl and stir in oil. Coat well. Stir in remaining ingredients. Allow to sit for 15 minutes and then serve immediately.

Shrimp and Penne Salad.

CHAPTER IV

Main Courses

From the simplest grilled or sautéed dishes to an elaborate molded turban, shrimp will star as the main course. Paired with less expensive fish or shellfish, or stretched with the addition of chicken, rice, or noodles, the delicate flavor of shrimp will highlight the recipe. Again, if you have a favorite meat or poultry recipe, adjust it to feature the ubiquitous shrimp to create an unforgettable meal.

ROCK HOUSE SHRIMP

SERVES 6.

1 large yellow bell pepper
1 large red bell pepper
½ cup dry white wine
3 cups heavy cream
2 tablespoons unsalted butter
¾ cup shelled unsalted pistachios
5 ounces sun-dried tomatoes
1 tablespoon minced fresh basil
1 teaspoon minced fresh parsley
1 pound soft goat cheese at room temperature
½ cup fine bread crumbs
24 jumbo shrimp, peeled, deveined, and butterflied (see page 11)
2 tablespoons olive oil
6 sprigs fresh basil (optional)

Place bell peppers over an open flame. Roast, turning frequently, until skin is blackened and peppers are slightly soft. Remove from flame and place in a tightly sealed plastic bag for about 10 minutes to allow peppers to steam. Remove from bag and gently push blackened skin off. Wipe any remaining black pieces off with a clean, damp cloth. Remove stem and seeds from peppers.

Chop yellow pepper and place in a small saucepan; chop red pepper and place in a second small saucepan. Add ¼ cup of wine to each saucepan. Place over medium heat and bring to a boil. Continue to boil for about 4 minutes or until liquid is reduced by half. Add 1½ cups heavy cream to each saucepan. Bring to a boil. When boiling, lower heat and simmer for about 20 minutes or until liquid is reduced by half. Remove from heat. Puree each of the pepper mixtures separately in a blender or food processor fitted with the metal blade. When pureed, add 1 tablespoon butter to each mixture, processing just to incorporate. Keep purees warm over hot water until ready to serve.

Preheat oven to 450°F.

Place the pistachios, sun-dried tomatoes, and herbs in a food processor fitted with the metal blade. Process, using quick on-and-off turns, until mixture is just chopped. Add the goat cheese and bread crumbs and process to blend. Place equal portions of the cheese mixture into the butterflied opening of each shrimp. Arrange stuffed shrimp, stuffed side up, on a lightly greased baking sheet with sides.

When all shrimp have been placed on baking sheet, drizzle tops with oil. Place the shrimp in the oven and bake for about 6 minutes or until shrimp are just cooked and cheese mixture is hot. Place equal portions of each sauce on 6 warm dinner plates, keeping each sauce separate but letting them meet in the center of the plates. Place 4 shrimp on each plate and garnish with a basil sprig, if desired. Serve immediately.

SHRIMP RISOTTO

SERVES 6 TO 8.

2 pounds shrimp, peeled and deveined
¼ cup unsalted butter
½ cup diced onions
½ cup diced fennel bulb
1½ tablespoons diced celery
1 tablespoon minced garlic
1 tablespoon minced fresh parsley
2 cups arborio rice*
½ cup dry white wine
Salt to taste
Pepper to taste
2 tablespoons minced fennel bulb tops
½ cup freshly grated Parmesan cheese
Available in Italian or gourmet markets.

Divide shrimp in half. Cut one half into bite-size pieces. Set aside. Finely mince remaining half and set aside.

Place 6 cups water in a heavy saucepan over high heat. Bring to a simmer.

Melt butter in a medium saucepan over medium-high heat. When melted, add onions, fennel bulb, and celery. Sauté for about 4 minutes or until vegetables are just softening. Stir in garlic and parsley. Bring to a boil. Cover and cook for 3 minutes. Uncover, add rice, and stir well to coat. When rice is glistening, add wine. Raise heat and bring to a boil, stirring constantly. Lower heat and continue to stir until wine has been absorbed, pushing rice from the sides and up from the bottom constantly. When the wine has evaporated completely, add a ladleful of the simmering water, stirring constantly. Continue adding a ladleful of water as the previous ladleful is absorbed. Never stop stirring.

After the rice has cooked for a total of 15 minutes, stir in minced shrimp, salt, and pepper. When the rice is about 5 minutes from being done, stir in the bite-size shrimp pieces. The rice will be done when the grains are still firm, but tender without chalkiness. The finished risotto should be slightly runny. To serve, stir in fennel tops and Parmesan.

KUNG PO SHRIMP

SERVES 6.

1½ pounds medium shrimp, peeled and deveined
¼ cup cornstarch
¼ cup red-wine vinegar
2 tablespoons rice-wine vinegar*
¼ cup light soy sauce
2 tablespoons sugar
¾ cup canola oil
6 small, dried red chili peppers
3 tablespoons minced fresh ginger
2 tablespoons minced garlic
1 teaspoon grated orange zest
2 cups tiny broccoli florets
¼ cup chopped scallions
   Warm cooked rice (optional)

Available in Asian or gourmet markets.

Rinse shrimp and pat dry. Toss with cornstarch.

Combine vinegars, soy sauce, and sugar in a nonreactive bowl. Set aside.

Heat oil in a wok over high heat. When hot, add the shrimp and stir-fry for about 2 minutes or until shrimp are just opaque. Remove shrimp and keep warm. Discard all but 2 tablespoons of the oil. Return wok to heat. When oil is hot, add chilies. Stir-fry for about 4 minutes or until chilies are black. (You may remove the chilies at this point, if desired.) Stir in ginger, garlic, orange zest, and broccoli, and stir-fry for 30 seconds. Add vinegar mixture and bring to a boil. When boiling, stir in shrimp. Stir-fry for about 1 minute or until shrimp are warmed through. Stir in scallions and serve immediately with rice, if desired.

Kung Po Shrimp served on a bed of rice.

LUCY'S SHRIMP ENCHILADAS

SERVES 6.

3 tablespoons vegetable oil
¾ cup chopped onions
¼ cup diced red bell peppers
¼ cup diced green bell peppers
1 New Mexico or other mildly hot chili pepper*, stemmed and chopped
1 tablespoon minced garlic
1 teaspoon minced fresh mint
1 teaspoon minced fresh basil
¼ teaspoon minced fresh oregano
1½ pounds small shrimp, peeled and deveined
1 cup peeled, seeded, and diced tomatoes
Salt to taste
Pepper to taste
1 cup grated Queso Blanco* or Monterey Jack cheese
12 flour tortillas
Enchilada Sauce
2 tablespoons chopped fresh cilantro
2 tablespoons chopped scallions

Available in Latin American or gourmet markets.

Heat oil in a heavy sauté pan over medium heat. When hot, add onions, peppers, chili, garlic, and herbs. Sauté, stirring frequently, for about 5 minutes or until vegetables are very soft. Add shrimp, tomatoes, salt, and pepper, stirring well to combine. Cook for about 4 minutes or until shrimp is firm and pink. Remove from heat. Taste and adjust seasoning with salt and pepper, if necessary.

Preheat oven to 350°F.

Lightly grease a 13-inch by 9-inch baking dish. Sprinkle 1 tablespoon cheese on each tortilla. Spoon equal portions of shrimp into the center of each tortilla. Fold over the edges and place each, seamside down, into the prepared dish. Nap with half of the Enchilada Sauce and sprinkle with the remaining cheese. Bake for about 10 minutes or until hot. Remove from the oven and serve immediately, sprinkled with cilantro and scallions. Serve with the remaining sauce on the side.

ENCHILADA SAUCE

MAKES ABOUT 4 CUPS.

6 tomatoes
3 ancho chili peppers
1 cup chopped onions
1 tablespoon minced garlic
1 tablespoon minced fresh cilantro
1 teaspoon minced fresh oregano
½ teaspoon ground cumin
½ teaspoon ground coriander
1 tablespoon white vinegar
1 tablespoon fresh lime juice
1 tablespoon tomato paste
1 teaspoon maple syrup

Preheat oven to 350°F.

Place tomatoes and chilies on a baking sheet in the oven. Bake for 20 minutes or until well roasted.

Skin, core, and seed tomatoes. Stem chilies. Place in a food processor fitted with the metal blade, add the remaining ingredients, and process until smooth. Pour into a medium saucepan over medium heat. Cook, stirring frequently, for 30 minutes or until it is quite thick and the flavors are blended.

This sauce may be made ahead and stored, covered and refrigerated, for up to 3 days.

MOM'S SHRIMP CREOLE

SERVES 6.

3 tablespoons unsalted butter or vegetable oil

3 tablespoons all-purpose flour

1 cup diced onions

½ cup diced celery

½ cup diced bell peppers

10 cloves garlic, peeled and minced

1½ teaspoons dried thyme

¼ teaspoon dried oregano

1 teaspoon chili powder

1 bay leaf

2 teaspoons Tabasco sauce (or to taste)

2½ cups diced canned tomatoes

½ cup water

1 tablespoon red-wine vinegar

Salt to taste

Pepper to taste

1½ pounds medium shrimp, peeled and deveined

1 cup frozen petit peas, thawed

6 to 8 cups warm cooked white rice

2 tablespoons minced parsley

If using butter, melt in a large, heavy saucepan over medium-high heat. Stir flour into melted butter or oil. Lower heat and cook roux, stirring constantly, for about 7 minutes or until golden brown. Add onions, celery, peppers, and garlic, and continue to cook for about 3 minutes or until vegetables are coated and beginning to soften. Stir in herbs, chili powder, bay leaf, and Tabasco. When well blended, add tomatoes, water, vinegar, salt, and pepper. Raise heat and bring to a boil, stirring constantly. Immediately lower heat and simmer for 20 minutes or until flavors are well blended and mixture has thickened. Remove bay leaf and stir in shrimp and peas. Cook for about 5 minutes or until shrimp has cooked through.

Place rice into serving bowls or onto a large serving platter. Pour shrimp creole over the rice and sprinkle with parsley. Serve immediately.

Mom's Shrimp Creole
served with rice and baking powder biscuits.

FILLET OF SOLE WITH SHRIMP MARGUÉRY

SERVES 6.

1½ pounds fillet of sole or other delicate
    white fish
2 cups fish stock (see page 12)
¾ pound small shrimp, peeled and deveined
1 cup shucked fresh oysters, well drained
½ cup unsalted butter, softened
¼ cup champagne or dry white wine
4 large egg yolks, slightly beaten
  Dash Tabasco sauce
  Salt to taste
  Pepper to taste
1 tablespoon minced fresh parsley

Preheat oven to 325°F.

Generously butter a shallow baking dish. Arrange the fish fillets in a single layer in the dish. Pour 1 cup fish stock over the top. Place shrimp and oysters on top of the fish. Cover lightly with aluminum foil. Bake for 15 minutes or until the fish is cooked through.

While the fish is cooking, place the remaining fish stock in the top half of double boiler over high heat. Boil until reduced to ¼ cup. Place top half of double boiler over bottom half of double boiler filled with hot water. Add butter and champagne or wine to the reduced fish stock and cook, stirring constantly, for about 3 minutes or until the butter has melted. Whisk in egg yolks and continue to whisk over hot, but not boiling, water for about 5 minutes or until the sauce has thickened. Whisk in Tabasco, salt, and pepper.

Remove the fish from the oven and turn oven temperature to broil. If desired, carefully transfer fish to an ovenproof serving platter. If leaving fish in the baking dish, drain off pan juices. Pour wine sauce over the cooked seafood. Place under broiler and broil for 3 minutes or until lightly browned. Serve immediately, sprinkled with parsley.

**Fillet of Sole with Shrimp Marguéry
served in an individual gratin dish.**

GARLIC SHRIMP WITH SAFFRON RICE

SERVES 6.

24 cloves garlic, roasted
   (see Note on page 66)
 1 cup Spanish olive oil
 1 cup Spanish sherry wine
 1 tablespoon minced fresh parsley
 1 teaspoon minced fresh tarragon
 1 teaspoon minced fresh marjoram
 ½ teaspoon grated lemon zest
 2 pounds small shrimp, peeled and deveined
   Saffron Rice

Push roasted garlic from skin into a small bowl. Whisk in oil, sherry, herbs, and lemon zest. Whisk until well combined.

Place shrimp in a shallow, nonreactive, ovenproof dish. Pour marinade over top and stir to coat well. Cover and refrigerate for at least 4 hours, stirring occasionally.

Preheat broiler.

Broil shrimp for about 5 minutes, turning once, or until cooked through and just beginning to crisp. Remove from heat.

Mound Saffron Rice on a warm serving platter. Pour shrimp and any juices over the rice and serve immediately.

SAFFRON RICE

MAKES ABOUT 3 ½ CUPS.

 2 tablespoons olive oil
 ¼ cup minced onions
 1 cup rice
 4 strands saffron
 3 cups hot unsalted, defatted chicken stock
   Salt to taste
   Pepper to taste
 ¼ cup minced fresh parsley
 ½ cup toasted slivered almonds

Preheat oven to 375°F.

Heat oil in a heavy, ovenproof casserole with cover over medium heat. When hot, stir in onions. Cook, stirring frequently, for about 4 minutes or until onions are soft. Stir in rice. Stir for about 2 minutes or until rice is well coated. Stir in saffron and stock. Add salt and pepper. Cover and bake for about 25 minutes or until rice is tender and liquid has been absorbed. Remove from oven. Stir in parsley and almonds. Serve hot.

CIOPPINO

SERVES 6.

1 tablespoon extra-virgin olive oil

½ cup diced onions

1 tablespoon minced garlic

4 cups diced canned Italian tomatoes (with juice)

½ cup dry red wine

2 tablespoons tomato paste

3 tablespoons minced fresh parsley

1 tablespoon minced fresh basil

1 teaspoon minced fresh thyme

½ teaspoon minced fresh oregano

¼ teaspoon red pepper flakes (or to taste)

Salt to taste

Pepper to taste

1 pound boneless, skinless fish chunks (halibut, cod, bass, sea trout)

1 pound small shrimp, peeled and deveined

12 to 15 clams and/or mussels, well scrubbed and in shells

Freshly grated Parmesan cheese

Garlic toast (optional)

Heat oil in a heavy saucepan over medium heat. When hot, add onions and garlic. Cook, stirring frequently, for about 4 minutes or until vegetables are softened but not brown. Stir in tomatoes, wine, tomato paste, herbs, red pepper flakes, salt, and pepper. Bring to a boil. When boiling, lower heat and simmer for 20 minutes. Stir in fish and cook for 5 minutes. Stir in shrimp and clams or mussels and cook for another 3 minutes or until clams or mussels have opened and shrimp are opaque.

Ladle into flat soup bowls. Sprinkle with Parmesan cheese and serve immediately with garlic toast, if desired.

GRILLED SHRIMP WITH WILD MUSHROOM RAGOUT

SERVES 6.

**24 jumbo shrimp, peeled, deveined, and
  butterflied (see page 11)**
1 cup dry white wine
2 tablespoons extra-virgin olive oil
1 tablespoon fresh lemon juice
1 tablespoon Tabasco sauce
2 tablespoons minced fresh marjoram
1 tablespoon minced garlic
1 tablespoon grated fresh ginger
  Salt to taste
  Pepper to taste
  Wild Mushroom Ragout

Place 4 shrimp on each of 6 skewers or push a wooden tooth-pick through each butterflied shrimp to hold them flat while grilling. Place in a shallow dish.

Combine wine, oil, lemon juice, Tabasco, marjoram, garlic, ginger, salt, and pepper. Pour over shrimp. Cover and refrigerate for 4 hours, turning occasionally.

Preheat grill or broiler.

Remove shrimp from marinade. Grill or broil for about 4 minutes or until shrimp are cooked and beginning to crisp. Remove from heat.

Place equal portions of Wild Mushroom Ragout on each of 6 dinner plates. Top each with 4 shrimp. Serve immediately.

WILD MUSHROOM RAGOUT

SERVES 6.

5 large portobello mushrooms
  (or other 3- to 4-inch diameter mushrooms)
3 tablespoons extra-virgin olive oil
1 tablespoon minced garlic
3 leeks, white parts only, washed and thinly
  sliced
1 tablespoon minced fresh marjoram
1 medium head radicchio, cored and
  julienned
  Salt to taste
  Pepper to taste
1 tablespoon balsamic vinegar

Trim stems from mushrooms. Wipe caps and stems clean. Slice the stems, but leave the caps whole.

Heat 2 tablespoons oil in a heavy sauté pan over medium-high heat. When hot, add mushroom caps, top side down. Sprinkle 1 tablespoon olive oil and garlic on gills. Cook for 4 minutes. Turn caps over and cook for an additional 3 minutes or until mushroom caps are cooked through. Remove to a bowl to drain. Keep the caps warm.

Add sliced stems, leeks, and marjoram to pan. Sauté for about 5 minutes or until soft. Stir in radicchio. Add salt and pepper and sauté for 3 minutes. Slice mushroom caps. Return sliced caps and any juices to the pan. Stir to combine with other vegetables. Stir in vinegar. When well combined, remove from heat and serve warm.

SHRIMP PIZZA

MAKES 1 12-INCH PIZZA.

- **½ pound large shrimp, peeled, deveined, and halved lengthwise**
- **1 tomato, peeled, seeded, and diced**
- **½ teaspoon salt**
- **1 tablespoon extra-virgin olive oil**
- **½ cup diced onions**
- **2 cloves garlic, peeled and minced**
- **1 unbaked 12-inch pizza round**
- **1 cup grated mozzarella cheese**
- **½ cup crumbled goat cheese**
- **6 pitted green olives, sliced**

Pat shrimp dry and set aside.

Place tomatoes in a colander. Sprinkle with salt and allow to drain for 30 minutes. Pat dry and set aside.

Preheat oven to 425°F.

Heat oil in heavy sauté pan over medium heat. When hot, add onions and garlic. Cook, stirring frequently, for about 4 minutes or until soft. Use a pastry brush to distribute oil, onions, and garlic on the pizza round. Sprinkle with mozzarella. Arrange shrimp decoratively on the mozzarella. Sprinkle with goat cheese, tomatoes, and olives.

Place prepared pizza on pizza stone and bake for 15 to 20 minutes or until crust is crisp. Serve hot.

Shrimp Pizza.

ANNAMARIE'S SHRIMP AND TOMATO SAUCE

SERVES 6.

- **1 tablespoon extra-virgin olive oil**
- **½ cup diced onions**
- **1 tablespoon minced garlic**
- **1 carrot, peeled and grated**
- **¼ cup vodka**
- **2 cans (28 ounces each) salt-free Italian plum tomatoes, chopped**
- **½ cup chopped fresh basil**
- **⅔ cup heavy cream**
- **1½ pounds medium shrimp, peeled and deveined**
- **2 tablespoons minced fresh parsley**
- **1 pound cooked rigatoni, penne, or other curled or tubular macaroni**

Heat oil in a heavy saucepan over medium heat. When hot, stir in onions, garlic, and carrot. Cook, stirring frequently, for about 4 minutes or until vegetables are soft. Add vodka. Raise heat and cook for 3 minutes. Add tomatoes and basil. Bring to a boil. Immediately lower heat and simmer for 15 minutes. Stir in cream and cook for 5 minutes. Add shrimp and parsley. Cook for 3 minutes, stirring occasionally, until shrimp are just pink. Stir in pasta and serve immediately.

OPEN-FACE SATURDAY NIGHT SHRIMP SANDWICHES WITH CARROT SALAD AND BLUE CHEESE DRESSING

SERVES 6.

1 avocado, peeled and seeded
Salt to taste
Juice of 1 lime (or to taste)
6 large slices sourdough or other crusty, coarse bread, lightly toasted
1 package radish or alfalfa sprouts
Carrot Salad
1½ pounds medium shrimp, shelled and deveined, grilled or deep-fried (see page 13)
Blue Cheese Dressing

Mash avocado. Stir in salt and lime juice.

Spread avocado on each slice of toast. Lightly mound radish or alfalfa sprouts on top of avocado. Sprinkle with Carrot Salad. Arrange shrimp over each one. Drizzle with Blue Cheese Dressing and serve immediately.

Open-Face Saturday Night Shrimp Sandwich with Carrot Salad and Blue Cheese Dressing served with marinated cherry tomatoes.

CARROT SALAD

MAKES ABOUT 2 CUPS.

1 large carrot, peeled and julienned
¼ cup julienned red onions
1 tablespoon fresh lemon juice
2 teaspoons brown sugar
½ teaspoon grated fresh ginger
¼ teaspoon cayenne pepper (or to taste)
Salt to taste

Place carrots in rapidly boiling water. Immediately remove from heat. Drain and refresh under cold running water. Pat dry. Combine with remaining ingredients. Allow to sit for 30 minutes. Taste and adjust seasoning, if necessary.

BLUE CHEESE DRESSING

MAKES ABOUT 3½ CUPS.

1½ cups creamed cottage cheese
¼ cup sour cream
2 tablespoons buttermilk
Tabasco sauce to taste
1½ cups crumbled Maytag Blue cheese or
other fine blue cheese

Process cottage cheese, sour cream, buttermilk, and Tabasco in a food processor fitted with the metal blade. When smooth, scrape into a serving bowl. Stir in blue cheese and allow to rest for 30 minutes before serving.

SHRIMP STEW

SERVES 6.

1 pound smoked hard sausage (such as kielbasa), cut into chunks
1½ pounds tiny new potatoes, washed
½ pound pearl onions, peeled
12 cloves garlic, peeled
2 tablespoons Shrimp Boil Spices (see page 124)
1 whole dried red chili pepper (or to taste)
1 teaspoon salt (or to taste)
6 ears fresh corn, husked and broken into thirds
2 pounds large or jumbo shrimp
Melted butter (optional)
Freshly grated horseradish (optional)

Bring about 2 gallons of water to a boil in a deep stockpot over high heat. When boiling, add sausage, potatoes, onions, garlic, Shrimp Boil Spices, chili, and salt. Return to a boil. Lower heat and simmer for 15 minutes. Add corn and cook for 8 minutes. Add shrimp and cook for about 4 minutes or until shrimp are opaque. Drain liquid from pot and serve sausage, vegetables, and shrimp heaped on a platter. Butter and horseradish can be poured over the top, if desired.

Shrimp Stew garnished with parsley.

SUNDAY NIGHT SHRIMP SUPPER WITH BAKING POWDER BISCUITS

SERVES 6.

3 ears fresh corn
1 pound small shrimp, peeled and deveined
¼ cup diced red bell peppers
2 tablespoons minced onions
1 cup milk
½ cup heavy cream
3 large eggs
1 tablespoon melted unsalted butter
½ teaspoon Tabasco sauce
   Salt to taste
   Pepper to taste
6 Baking Powder Biscuits

Preheat oven to 350°F.

Cut corn kernels from ears, scraping to extract all liquid from ears. Combine with all remaining ingredients except biscuits in an ovenproof casserole. Cover with foil and bake for 30 minutes. Remove foil and place biscuits on top. Return to oven. Raise heat to 450°F and bake for 15 minutes or until biscuits are golden and casserole is set. Serve hot.

BAKING POWDER BISCUITS

MAKES ABOUT 12 BISCUITS.

2¼ cups all-purpose flour
1 tablespoon finely ground cornmeal
4 teaspoons baking powder
1 teaspoon sugar (or to taste) or salt to taste
⅓ cup vegetable shortening
   About ⅔ cup milk

Place flour, cornmeal, baking powder, and sugar or salt in a food processor fitted with the metal blade. Use quick on-and-off turns to combine. Add shortening and continue processing with on-and-off turns until just combined. With the motor running, add enough milk to make a soft dough; do not overprocess. Turn out onto a lightly floured board. Pat down and smooth edges to form a ¾-inch-thick circle. Cut out circles using a 2-inch biscuit cutter or drinking glass. Bake dough circles as directed in Sunday Night Shrimp Supper.

Note: To bake biscuits alone, place 1 tablespoon butter or margarine in a cast-iron skillet or baking pan. Place in a preheated 450°F oven and allow to melt. When butter is melted and the pan is hot, add biscuits with all sides touching. Bake for about 12 minutes or until lightly brown and slightly raised. Serve hot.

SHRIMP FRIED RICE

SERVES 6.

2 tablespoons oyster sauce*
2 tablespoons soy sauce
1 tablespoon rice wine* or dry white wine
2 teaspoons sesame oil*
2 teaspoons grated fresh ginger
1 teaspoon sugar
½ pound medium shrimp, peeled, deveined, and cut into small pieces
3 large eggs
Salt to taste
White pepper to taste
2 tablespoons canola oil
1 cup finely diced Virginia ham
1 teaspoon minced garlic
¼ cup frozen petit peas, thawed
6 water chestnuts, diced
6 cups cold cooked long-grain rice
3 scallions, washed, trimmed, and sliced
Available in Asian or gourmet markets.

Whisk together the oyster sauce, 1 tablespoon soy sauce, wine, sesame oil, ginger, and sugar. Pour over shrimp in a nonreactive bowl and stir to coat. Cover and refrigerate for 1 hour.

Beat eggs with salt and pepper. Heat 1 tablespoon canola oil in a wok over high heat. When hot, whisk in eggs and stir-fry, breaking into pieces as you scramble. When eggs are scrambled, remove from wok and keep warm. Wipe wok clean.

Heat 1 teaspoon canola oil in the wok over high heat. When hot, stir in ham and garlic. Stir-fry for about 30 seconds. Remove from wok and keep warm. Wipe wok clean.

Heat 1 teaspoon canola oil in the wok over high heat. When hot, stir in marinated shrimp, peas, and water chestnuts. Stir-fry for about 2 minutes or until shrimp is just beginning to cook. Remove from wok and keep warm. Do not wipe wok clean.

Heat 1 teaspoon canola oil in the wok over high heat. When hot, stir in rice and stir-fry for about 3 minutes or until rice is beginning to color. Stir in eggs, ham and garlic, and shrimp mixture. Stir-fry for about 30 seconds. Add remaining soy sauce and scallions, and stir-fry for an additional 30 seconds. Serve the fried rice immediately.

SHRIMP TEMPURA WITH DIPPING SAUCE

SERVES 6.

1½ to 2 pounds large shrimp, peeled and
   deveined, tails intact
1 cup all-purpose flour
2 teaspoons baking powder
1 large egg
½ teaspoon salt
¼ teaspoon sugar
1 cup ice water
   About 6 cups vegetable oil
   Dipping Sauce
   Pickled ginger*
*Available in Asian or gourmet markets.

Butterfly shrimp as directed on page 11.

Combine flour, baking powder, egg, salt, sugar, and ice water until just moistened. Don't overmix. Batter should be lumpy.

Heat oil in a deep-fryer, wok, or saucepan over high heat until it reaches 375°F on a food thermometer. Pat shrimp dry and dip, by the tail, into batter. Drop into hot oil, a few at a time, and fry for about 2 to 3 minutes or until golden. Drain on paper towels and serve immediately with Dipping Sauce and pickled ginger.

Note: Traditionally, shrimp tempura is served with tempura vegetables as well. You can lessen the amount of shrimp per serving and add tempura batter-fried thinly sliced carrots, sweet potatoes, beets, squash, asparagus spears, whole small mushrooms, green beans, artichoke hearts, taro root, or any other vegetable you like.

DIPPING SAUCE

MAKES ABOUT 1 ¼ CUPS.

1 cup light soy sauce
¼ cup sake* or dry sherry
2 teaspoons grated fresh ginger
¼ teaspoon wasabi powder*
**2 scallions, washed, trimmed, and finely
   sliced**

*Available in Asian or gourmet markets.

Place soy sauce, sake or sherry, ginger, and wasabi powder in a small saucepan over high heat. Bring to a boil. Remove from heat and allow to sit for 15 minutes. Strain into a serving bowl. Stir in scallions and serve at room temperature.

SHRIMP ETOUFFEE

SERVES 6.

¼ cup unsalted butter
3 tablespoons all-purpose flour
¼ cup finely diced onions
¼ cup finely diced celery
2 tablespoons minced garlic
½ cup fish stock (see page 12)
½ cup water
2 tablespoons minced parsley
1 teaspoon cayenne pepper (or to taste)
Salt to taste
**1½ pounds medium shrimp, peeled and
   deveined**
1 teaspoon fresh lime juice
Warm cooked rice (optional)

Melt butter in a heavy saucepan over medium-high heat. When melted, stir in flour and cook, stirring constantly, for about 5 minutes or until flour is deep golden-brown. Stir in onions, celery, and garlic. Continue to stir for 5 more minutes. Whisk in stock and water. When well blended, add parsley, cayenne, and salt. Cook for 5 minutes.

   Stir in shrimp. Cover and cook for 5 to 8 minutes or until sauce is thick and flavors are blended. Stir in lime juice. Serve alone or over rice, if desired.

STIR-FRIED SHRIMP WITH GINGER NOODLES

SERVES 6.

1 cup white wine

¼ cup rice-wine vinegar*

3 teaspoons sesame oil*

1 teaspoon grated fresh ginger

2 cloves garlic, peeled and minced

1 serrano chili pepper, seeded and minced

1 tablespoon light brown sugar

1½ pounds medium shrimp, peeled and deveined

1 package (1 pound) capellini or angel-hair pasta

¼ cup julienned pickled ginger*

¼ cup sliced scallions

2 tablespoons minced fresh cilantro

1 tablespoon cornstarch

¼ cup water

***Available in Asian or gourmet markets.**

Combine wine, vinegar, 1 teaspoon oil, ginger, garlic, chili, and brown sugar. Pour over the shrimp and allow them to marinate for 1 hour.

Cook pasta as directed on package until al dente. Remove from heat and drain well. When well drained, toss with remaining oil, pickled ginger, scallions, and cilantro. Keep warm.

Dissolve cornstarch in water. Heat a wok over high heat. When hot, pour in shrimp mixture and quickly stir-fry for about 3 minutes or until shrimp are just cooked. Add cornstarch mixture and stir until sauce is thickened. Immediately pour over noodles, toss to coat, and serve.

Stir-Fried Shrimp with Ginger Noodles.

SHRIMP GRITS WITH MUSTARD CREAM

SERVES 6.

4 cups cooked grits
3 large eggs
1 cup grated fontina cheese
1 cup heavy cream
¼ teaspoon ground nutmeg
Pinch cayenne pepper
1 pound cooked shrimp, peeled, deveined, and chopped
1 cup diced cooked bacon or ham
1 tablespoon melted unsalted butter
Mustard Cream

Preheat oven to 350°F.

Grease a 2-quart casserole.

Combine grits, eggs, cheese, cream, nutmeg, and cayenne. When well combined, stir in shrimp and bacon or ham bits. Pour into the prepared casserole. Brush with butter. Place the casserole in an ovenproof baking dish and pour in enough boiling water to come halfway up all sides of the casserole. Bake for about 25 minutes or until set. Serve hot with Mustard Cream.

MUSTARD CREAM

MAKES ABOUT 1¼ CUPS.

1 cup heavy cream
¼ cup coarse-grain mustard
1 teaspoon fresh lime juice

Bring cream to a boil in a small saucepan over medium-high heat. Cook at a low boil for about 10 minutes or until cream is slightly thickened and coats the back of a spoon. Stir in mustard and lime juice and serve immediately or keep warm over hot water until ready to use.

MOLDED SEAFOOD TURBAN WITH CURRY CREAM SAUCE

SERVES 6 TO 8.

4 tablespoons unsalted butter, softened
2½ pounds boneless white fish fillets
2 tablespoons fresh lemon juice
2 tablespoons fresh orange juice
Salt to taste
White pepper to taste
1 pound shrimp, peeled and deveined
2 large egg whites
1 cup heavy cream
2 tablespoons cognac
1 teaspoon minced fresh tarragon
1 teaspoon minced fresh parsley
1 teaspoon minced fresh thyme
¼ teaspoon Tabasco sauce
Curry Cream Sauce
½ cup watercress leaves

Preheat oven to 350°F.

Using 2 tablespoons butter, generously butter a 5-cup ring mold.

Pat fillets dry. Combine citrus juices and sprinkle over both sides of the fillets. Season with salt and pepper.

Line the mold with fillets, narrow ends to the center, leaving an overhang on both the inside and outside edges. If the fillets have a dark side, place the dark side up.

Place shrimp, egg whites, cream, cognac, herbs, 1 tablespoon butter, Tabasco, and salt in a food processor fitted with the metal blade. Process until smooth. When smooth, scrape into the fish-lined mold and tamp down. Fold fillet overhang to enclose shrimp puree. Pat down to firmly cover. Melt remaining tablespoon of butter and brush onto the fillets. Make a tent of aluminum foil to fit over the top of the mold, but do not let it touch the top of the fish. Place the mold in an ovenproof baking dish and pour in enough boiling water to come up 1 inch around the mold. Bake for 30 minutes or until just cooked through. Remove from oven and carefully loosen edges of mold with a sharp knife.

Invert on heated serving platter to unmold. Spoon Curry Cream Sauce over top. Sprinkle with watercress and serve the seafood turban immediately.

OVEN-BARBECUED SHRIMP

SERVES 6.

2 pounds large shrimp
½ cup butter
2 tablespoons bottled chili sauce
1 tablespoon Worcestershire sauce
1 tablespoon fresh orange juice
1 tablespoon fresh lemon juice
1 teaspoon maple syrup
2 cloves garlic, peeled and minced
1 teaspoon minced fresh parsley
¼ teaspoon cayenne pepper

Cut shrimp shells down the center back, leaving shells on. Place in a single layer in a shallow baking dish. Combine butter, chili sauce, Worcestershire sauce, citrus juices, syrup, garlic, parsley, and cayenne in a small saucepan over medium heat. Cook for 5 minutes or until well combined. Pour over shrimp. Cover and refrigerate for at least 3 hours.

Preheat oven to 350°F.

Bake shrimp for 12 minutes or until well cooked and starting to crisp. Serve immediately.

Note: The shrimp can also be placed on skewers and grilled (see page 13).

Oven-Barbecued Shrimp
garnished with parsley and lemon wedge.

CURRY CREAM SAUCE

MAKES ABOUT 1½ CUPS.

¼ cup unsalted butter
¼ cup all-purpose flour
1 tablespoon curry powder
½ teaspoon salt
¼ teaspoon white pepper
¼ teaspoon grated orange zest
1 cup heavy cream, warmed
2 large egg yolks, beaten
¼ cup sherry
1 tablespoon fresh lemon juice

Melt butter in top half of a double boiler over boiling water. When melted, whisk in flour, curry powder, salt, pepper, and orange zest. When well combined, whisk in cream. Cook, stirring constantly, for about 5 minutes or until thick.

Whisk a small amount of thickened cream sauce into beaten egg yolks. When well blended, whisk yolks back into sauce. Whisk in sherry and continue to cook, stirring constantly, for about 5 minutes or until the sauce is hot and quite thick. Stir in lemon juice. Serve immediately or keep warm over hot water until ready to use.

SIMPLE SHRIMP CURRY

SERVES 6.

⅓ cup clarified butter (see Note on page 35)
1 cup diced onions
1 tablespoon minced fresh ginger
1 tablespoon minced garlic
¼ cup curry powder
1 teaspoon cayenne pepper (or to taste)
¾ cup coconut milk*
1 cup fish stock (see page 12) or clam juice
½ cup mango puree
½ cup heavy cream
1 tablespoon fresh lemon juice
Salt to taste
Pepper to taste
1½ pounds medium shrimp, peeled and deveined
¼ cup unflavored yogurt
1 cup toasted cashew halves
4 to 6 cups warm cooked rice

Available in Indian or gourmet markets.

Heat butter in a heavy saucepan over medium heat. When hot, add onions and fry, stirring frequently, for about 20 minutes or until onions are deep red-brown. Lower heat if onions are browning too quickly. Do not allow to burn.

Stir in ginger and garlic, and cook for 3 minutes. Add curry powder, cayenne, and coconut milk. Cook for about 2 minutes until well incorporated. Add fish stock or clam juice, mango puree, cream, lemon juice, salt, and pepper, and cook for about 15 minutes or until sauce is slightly thickened. Stir in shrimp and cook for 5 minutes or until shrimp is cooked through. Stir in yogurt, a tablespoon at a time. Add cashews and serve over rice.

Simple Shrimp Curry served over steamed rice
and garnished with cilantro leaves.

CHAPTER V

Spices and Sauce Mixes

In addition to the sauces included in this chapter, you can use flavored mayonnaises or exotic mustards to make other tasty sauces for shrimp. For instance, to each cup of mayonnaise you might want to add ¼ cup minced fresh herbs; or 2 tablespoons minced fresh garlic; or 1 teaspoon dry mustard, ½ teaspoon cayenne pepper, and 1 teaspoon fresh lemon juice; or 2 teaspoons curry powder, 1 teaspoon canola oil, 1 tablespoon fresh lime juice, 1 tablespoon minced fresh cilantro, and minced chili peppers to taste; or any other flavoring you particularly love. There are many exotic commercially prepared mustards that could also enhance the flavor of shrimp.

STANDARD COCKTAIL SAUCE

MAKES ABOUT 1¼ CUPS.

1 cup bottled chili sauce
2 tablespoons well-drained bottled horseradish (or to taste)
1 tablespoon fresh lemon juice
1 teaspoon Tabasco sauce
½ teaspoon Worcestershire sauce

Combine all ingredients. Cover and refrigerate until ready to serve. Use as a condiment with cold cooked shrimp.

A tray of sauces (clockwise from top left): Cocktail, Cucumber, Tartar, Lemon, and Rémoulade.

REMOULADE SAUCE

MAKES ABOUT 2 CUPS.

2 large hard-boiled eggs, peeled and chopped
1½ cups mayonnaise
2 tablespoons minced fresh parsley
1 tablespoon minced garlic
1 tablespoon freshly grated horseradish
1 tablespoon white-wine vinegar
2 teaspoons dry mustard
½ teaspoon paprika
Dash hot-pepper sauce
Salt to taste
White pepper to taste

Place all ingredients in a blender or food processor fitted with the metal blade and process until smooth and creamy. Scrape into a nonreactive container. Cover and refrigerate at least 2 hours before using. Use as a condiment with cold cooked shrimp or as a dressing in shrimp salads.

TARTAR SAUCE

MAKES ABOUT 1 ½ CUPS.

1 cup mayonnaise
½ cup finely chopped cornichons or dill pickles
2 tablespoons chopped capers
1 tablespoon fresh lemon juice
1 tablespoon minced onions
1 clove garlic, peeled and minced
1 teaspoon minced fresh parsley
1 teaspoon Dijon-style mustard

Combine all ingredients. When well blended, cover and refrigerate for at least 1 hour before serving. Use as a condiment with fried shrimp or cold cooked shrimp.

CUCUMBER SAUCE

MAKES ABOUT 1 ½ CUPS.

1 cup sour cream or crème fraîche*
½ cup peeled, seeded, and grated cucumber
1 tablespoon minced fresh dill
1 teaspoon minced fresh chives
½ teaspoon Tabasco sauce (or to taste)
  Salt to taste
Available in gourmet markets.

Combine all ingredients. Place in a nonreactive container. Cover and refrigerate for at least 1 hour before using. Use as a condiment with cold cooked shrimp or as a dressing in shrimp salads.

BEURRE BLANC (OR BEURRE ROUGE)

MAKES 1 CUP.

¼ cup white (or red) wine
3 tablespoons white-wine vinegar (or red-
   wine vinegar)
1 tablespoon fresh lemon juice
3 tablespoons minced fresh shallots
½ pound chilled unsalted butter, cubed
   Salt to taste

Combine wine, vinegar, lemon juice, and shallots in a nonreactive saucepan over very low heat. Cook until all liquid has evaporated and shallots are mushy. Watch the pan carefully so the mixture does not scorch. Remove from heat and whisk in 2 cubes of butter. When butter has melted, return to very low heat and continue to carefully whisk in butter, a cube at a time, adding a new cube just as the previous one has melted, until a smooth sauce has formed. Remove from heat if the butter separates and whisk rapidly to reemulsify the sauce. Whisk in salt and serve immediately, or hold in the top half of a double boiler over hot water until ready to serve. Serve the sauce over warm poached or sautéed shrimp.

LEMON SAUCE

MAKES ABOUT ¾ CUP.

2 tablespoons fresh lemon juice
½ teaspoon grated lemon zest
¾ teaspoon dry mustard
¼ teaspoon freshly grated horseradish
½ cup chilled unsalted butter, cubed
¼ cup unflavored yogurt

Place lemon juice in a small, nonreactive saucepan over very low heat. Cook until reduced by half. Stir in lemon zest, mustard, and horseradish. When well blended, carefully whisk in butter, a cube at a time, adding a new cube just as the previous one has melted, until a smooth sauce has formed. Remove from heat if butter separates and whisk rapidly to reemulsify the sauce. Whisk in yogurt and serve the sauce immediately over warm poached shrimp.

TERIYAKI MARINADE

MAKES ABOUT 2 CUPS.

1 cup light soy sauce
¼ cup rice-wine vinegar*
1 tablespoon fresh lime juice
1 tablespoon fresh orange juice
1 tablespoon dark rum
2 tablespoons grated fresh ginger
2 teaspoons minced garlic
1 teaspoon honey
¼ teaspoon minced hot chili peppers
   (optional)
½ cup water
***Available in Asian or gourmet markets.**

Combine all ingredients except the water. When well combined, whisk in the water. Pour over shrimp or other fish or meat, cover, and marinate for at least 1 hour before grilling, sautéing, or baking.

SHRIMP BOIL SPICES

MAKES ABOUT ¾ CUP.

6 whole dried red chili peppers
24 whole cloves
¼ cup mustard seeds
3 tablespoons black peppercorns
8 bay leaves
6 allspice berries
1 tablespoon celery seeds
1 teaspoon dried tarragon
1 teaspoon coriander seeds
1 teaspoon fennel seeds
½ teaspoon dried thyme
1 tablespoon grated orange zest
1 tablespoon grated lemon zest

Combine all ingredients. Store, covered and refrigerated, for up to 3 months. Two tablespoons tied in a cheesecloth bag will season 1 gallon of water well.

BARBECUE SPICE RUB

MAKES ABOUT ²/₃ CUP.

¼ cup chili powder
2 tablespoons paprika
1 tablespoon light brown sugar
2 teaspoons ground cumin
1 teaspoon ground coriander
½ teaspoon dry mustard
¼ teaspoon dried oregano
¼ teaspoon cayenne pepper (or to taste)
¼ teaspoon ground cinnamon
¼ teaspoon onion powder
1 tablespoon salt (or to taste)
1 teaspoon pepper (or to taste)

Combine all ingredients. Cover and store for up to 3 months in a cool, dry spot. Generously coat shrimp with Barbecue Spice Rub before grilling or barbecuing.

CAJUN SPICE RUB

MAKES ABOUT ½ CUP.

2 tablespoons paprika
1 tablespoon cayenne pepper
1 tablespoon unsalted onion powder
1 tablespoon unsalted garlic powder
1 teaspoon dried lemon peel
1 teaspoon black pepper
1 teaspoon white pepper
1 teaspoon salt
1 teaspoon dried oregano
1 teaspoon dried thyme
1 teaspoon ground fennel
½ teaspoon ground cumin
¼ teaspoon crushed dried bay leaf

Combine all ingredients. Cover and store for up to 3 months in a cool, dry spot. Generously coat shrimp with Cajun Spice Rub before grilling or barbecuing.

INDEX

Annamarie's Shrimp and
    Tomato Sauce, 101
Appetizers, 15–47
Avocado, 22, 61

Barbecue Spice Rub, 125
Beans, black, 71
Black Bean and Shrimp Salad,
    70, 71
Blue Cheese Shrimp, 32
Brochettes of Shrimp and
    Papaya, 47

Cajun Spice Rub, 125
Cheese, 32, 104
Cioppino, 97
Coconut, 23
Coconut Shrimp with Ginger
    Dipping Sauce, 23
Cold Avocado and Shrimp
    Soup, *60*, 61
Couscous, 77
Crepes, 34–35
Crunchy Buttermilk Shrimp
    Soup, 52
Curries
    Curry Cream Sauce, 114
    Red Curry, 56
    Simple Shrimp Curry, 117

Dressings
    Blue Cheese, 104
    Mustard Cream, 112
    Spicy Cream Cheese, 73
    Tomato Dressing, 66
Dumplings, 29–30

Entrees, 85–117

Fillet of Sole with Shrimp
    Marguéry, 94, *95*
Fruit, 47

Garlic Shrimp with Saffron
    Rice, 96
Ginger, 23, 42–43, 111
Greek Shrimp Salad, 64, *65*
Grilled Shrimp with Wild
    Mushroom Ragout,
    98–99

Hors d'Oeuvres, 15–47

Italian Seafood Salad, 75

Jellied Shrimp Madrilène, 59

Kung Po Shrimp, 88, *89*

Lemon Grass and Shrimp
    Soup with Red Curry,
    56–57
Lentils, 57
Lucy's Shrimp Enchiladas,
    90–91

Main courses, 85–117
Molded Seafood Turban with
    Curry Cream Sauce,
    113–114
Mom's Shrimp Creole, *92*, 93

New York Parties Shrimp
    Dijon, 41
Noodles, 81, 111

Open-Face Saturday Night
    Shrimp Sandwiches with
    Carrot Salad and Blue
    Cheese Dressing, *102*,
    103
Oven-Barbecued Shrimp, 114,
    115

Papaya, 47
Pesto, 19
Pickled Shrimp, *40*, 41

Poached Shrimp with Poblano
    Pesto, 19
Potted Shrimp, 17
Prosciutto, 18

Rice
    fried, 107
    risotto, 87
    saffron, 96
    wild, 78
Rock House Shrimp, 86
Rubie's Carolina Shrimp
    Salad, 66
Rubs, 125

Salads, 63–83, 103
Sauces
    Avgolemono Sauce, 61
    Avocado Dill Sauce, 22
    Beurre Blanc, 123
    Chili Sauce, 45
    Cocktail Sauce, 121
    Cucumber Sauce, 122
    Curry Cream Sauce, 114
    Dipping Sauce, 31, 109
    Enchilada Sauce, 91
    Garlic Sauce, 27
    Ginger Dipping Sauce, 23

INDEX

Ginger Sauce, 42, 43
Lemon Sauce, 123
Poblano Pesto, 19
Rémoulade Sauce, 121
Spicy Dipping Sauce, 39
Tartar Sauce, 122
Vodka Sauce, 35
Wild Mushroom Ragout, 99
Sautéed Shrimp Salad with
    Tarragon Balsamic
    Vinaigrette, 79
Seafood Chef's Salad, *74*, 75
Shrimp and Couscous Salad,
    76, 77
Shrimp and Lentil Soup, 57
Shrimp and Penne Salad, 82,
    83
Shrimp And Tomato Aspic
    with Spicy Cream
    Cheese, 72–73
Shrimp basics
    boiled, 12
    butterflying, 11, *11*
    buying, 9
    cooking, 12–13
    deep-fried, 13
    deveining, 10, *10*
    grilled, 13

preparing, 10–11
sauteed, 13
shelling, 10, *10*
Shrimp Bisque, 58
Shrimp Boil, 13, 124
Shrimp Butter, 17
Shrimp Caesar Salad, 67
Shrimp Canapes, 45
Shrimp Cocktail, *16*, 17
Shrimp Crostini, 33
Shrimp Cuernavaca, 24
Shrimp Dumplings with
    Dipping Sauce, *28*, 29,
    30, *30*
Shrimp Étouffée, 109
Shrimp-Filled Tomato Crepes
    with Peppered Vodka
    Sauce, 34–35
Shrimp Fried Rice, 107
Shrimp Fritters with Garlic
    Sauce, 27
Shrimp Gazpacho, *54*, 55
Shrimp Grits with Mustard
    Cream, 112
Shrimp in Tomato Dressing,
    66
Shrimp Louis, 73
Shrimp Minestrone, 53
Shrimp Nachos, 22

Shrimp Pan Roast, 26
Shrimp Pâté with Avocado Dill
    Sauce, *20*, 21
Shrimp Pizza, *100*, 101
Shrimp Rémoulade, 67
Shrimp Risotto, 87
Shrimp Scampi, 31
Shrimp Soup with
    Avgolemono Sauce, 61
Shrimp Spring Rolls with Spicy
    Dipping Sauce, *36*,
    37–39
Shrimp Stew, 104, *105*
Shrimp Tempura with Dipping
    Sauce, 108–109
Shrimp Timbales with Fresh
    Ginger Sauce, 42
Shrimp Toast, 46
Shrimp with Snow Peas and
    Prosciutto, 18
Simple Shrimp Chowder, 50,
    51
Simple Shrimp Curry, *116*,
    117
Snow Peas, 18
Soba Noodle Salad with
    Shrimp and Pickled
    Ginger, *80*, 81
Soups, 49–61

Spicy Shrimp Pancakes with
    Chili Sauce, 44
Spinach, 50
Spinach and Shrimp Soup, 50
Stir-Fried Shrimp with Ginger
    Noodles, 111, *112*
Sunday Night Shrimp Supper
    with Baking Powder
    Biscuits, 106

Tempura, 108
Teriyaki Marinade, 124
Thai Shrimp and Peanut
    Salad, 68, *69*
Toasted Almond Shrimp
    Salad, 82
Tuscan Shrimp Salad, 77

Vegetables
    avocado, 22, 61
    black beans, 71
    lentils, 57
    snow peas, 18
    spinach, 50

Warm Shrimp Salad, 64
Wild Rice and Shrimp Salad,
    78

THE UBIQUITOUS SHRIMP

Sources

Page 16: glass and dish, Williams-Sonoma

Page 20: platter, Pfaltzgraff

Page 25: salt and pepper shakers, Williams-Sonoma

Page 28: bamboo steamer, Williams-Sonoma

Page 50: dishes and spoon, the L.S. Collection; tureen, Williams-Sonoma; salt and pepper shakers, Pottery Barn

Page 54: all dinnerware, Pottery Barn

Page 60: fabric designed by Janice Brown for Covington; dinnerware, Pfaltzgraff; spoon, Pottery Barn

Page 64: platter, Pfaltzgraff; salad servers, Pottery Barn

Page 69: platter and serving pieces, the L.S. Collection

Page 74: platter, Williams-Sonoma

Page 76: plate, cup and saucer, flatware, the L.S. Collection

Page 83: plates, the L.S. Collection; salt and pepper shakers, Williams-Sonoma

Page 92: plate and bowl, Pfaltzgraff

Page 95: baking dish, Williams-Sonoma; plate, cup and saucer, the L.S. Collection

Page 100: fabric designed by Janice Brown for Covington

Page 105: platter, Pfaltzgraff

Page 116: platter, Pfaltzgraff; serving pieces, Pottery Barn

Private collections: pages 36, 40, 80, 89, 102, 110, 115, 120

ADDRESSES

Janice Brown
267 Fifth Avenue
New York, N.Y. 10016

Pottery Barn
700 Broadway
New York, N.Y. 10003
(212) 505-6377

The Pfaltzgraff Company
225 Fifth Avenue
New York, N.Y. 10010

Williams-Sonoma
20 East 60th Street
New York, N.Y. 10022
(212) 780-5155

The L.S. Collection
765 Madison Avenue
New York, N.Y. 10021
(212) 472-3355